DREAM

Destiny Fulfilled By Grace

"Disrupting expectations to make your dreams become your reality."

ROMELO PUBLICATIONS

Written By
Award Winning Entrepreneur & Business Strategist

Victoria A. Morgan

DREAM. Destiny Fulfilled by Grace
Copyright @ 2019 by Victoria A. Morgan

This title is also available as an ebook. ISBN 978-1-9990430-1-8

Requests for information should be addressed to:

Romelo Publications
406-134 Queen Street East
Brampton, ON. Canada
L6V 1B2

This softcover edition: ISBN 978-1-9990430-0-1

Romelo Publications 2019

Library and Archives Canada:

Morgan, Victoria A.
DREAM. Destiny Fulfilled by Grace: acquiring blind faith to manifest your purpose
Includes footnote references.
ISBN 978-1-9990430-0-1
1. Christian Life
2. Spiritual Growth

The Scriptures cited in this book are footnoted and becomes a part of this copyright page.

Any information, data, and references are offered as a resource. They are not intended in any way to be or imply an endorsement by Romelo Publications.

Cover design:
Interior design: Cre8tive Eye Designs

*This book is dedicated to my children,
Roshawn, Malachi, and London.
Keep your dreams alive and never give up until
you accomplish them.
Always remember that a dream deferred is not a dream denied.*

Mommy loves you.

Table Of Content

Acknowledgements:

Writing a book is no easy task. It cannot be done without the help and support of others. For this reason, I need to acknowledge the following people:

My editor, Talia Leacock-Campbell, who always has the right words for what I want to say. Without her commitment and service, this book would not have been completed.

Special thanks to my greatest support and my brother Romeo Morgan who has encouraged me and motivated me when I became lackadaisical.

And to my Sisters in Christ, Angella Taylor-Anderson, Tanasha Smith, and Stephanie Martin, who contributed, answered questions, provided insights, and shared their experiences and words of encouragement in this book. No one could ask for better sister friends. I love you all unconditionally.

An extra special thanks to my spiritual mentor and coach, Pastor Tanya Baker, who spoke over my life and said I needed to write this book.

But most of all, I need to thank my late grandparents, Roy and Inez Darby, because without them to support, guide and keep my dreams alive, none of this would even exist. My life is what it is today because of you both. Sleep well!

Leacock-Campbell, who always has the right words for what I want to say. Without her commitment and service, this book would not have been completed.

Special thanks to my greatest support and my brother Romeo Morgan who has encouraged me and motivated me when I became lackadaisical.

Introduction:

"God doesn't want us to merely sit around dreaming about things we can do and be. That's a good place to start, but a poor place to stop. God wants us to turn our dreams into action."
– Victoria Osteen

This book you hold in your hands and all the stories it contains are a testament to the unrivalled power of God's grace. There were so many points in my life where pursuing my dreams seemed impossible. There were days I questioned how I could dare to dream so big? What right did I have to chase my goals? And when obstacles cropped up and stunted my progress, I wondered if perhaps my dreams were only meant to exist in my head. From legal trouble to single motherhood, family traumas to troubling career paths, the setbacks seemed endless.

But every time I tried to shrink back from the dream that kept calling out to me through the chaos of my life, I was gently pushed back in the direction of my goals. Each time I was derailed and I was tempted to give up on my vision, I found myself always back on the path towards a dream that was planted in my heart and mind as a child. I know now that the voice I kept hearing and the push I kept feeling were because my dreams weren't just mine, they were God's vision for my life. As I write these words today, I live a life I never thought imaginable, all thanks to God's perfect plan and his boundless grace.

I felt compelled to write this book because I want you to experience the pure joy of discovering and pursuing the life that God has selected for you. It is no coincidence that you feel the call to do more, to be more, and to aim higher, even when all the circumstances in your life suggest that you shouldn't. It's not by mistake that you keep hearing that call—whether it's a tiny whisper or a roaring shout—to chase the dream you just can't shake.

I know that you might doubt your worthiness, strength, and abilities. You may be feeling discouraged by a path that seems littered with challenges. It might feel like you'll never catch a break. But I want to assure you that God chose you for the dream he's placed on your heart, not so that it can hide away in your imagination, but so that you can live it out loud. God knows your potential, and there is no path that he cannot clear.

Inside the pages of this book are the stories of how God's grace has brought me through the most dire of circumstances, how faith rescued me from my darkest moments, and the lessons and scriptures that guided me towards a life where my dreams—even the biggest ones—become my reality. Because you deserve to do more than dream about the things you can be and do. You deserve to see your dreams become a reality, no matter how impossible and lofty they might seem. And you deserve to know that God's Word, love, and grace are the ultimate guide to a life of contentment, purpose, and fulfillment.

I pray that by the time you reach the end of this book, that you begin to not just walk toward your dreams, but to run full speed, trusting God's perfect vision to carry you over every obstacle and through any challenge. Welcome to your new life of destiny fulfilled by grace.

Your sister in dreams and faith,
Victoria A. Morgan

PART I:

FINDING DESTINY

DREAM

Chapter One:
LOCK IN

My dream of being a lawyer first came to me early one morning when I was in the third grade. That morning, like every other, I sat at the window of my classroom, watching for my friend to arrive. I was always early, so it wasn't unusual that I was there before him, but something felt very different. There was just something uneasy about that morning, and I knew something was wrong.

My worst nightmare came true when the teacher came into the class and told us that my friend had been struck while crossing the street. I felt my heart collapse as I struggled for air. He was my best friend. We spoke about everything. He would listen to me when I was sad and always had the right words to say. When I learned that the driver who struck him did not stop, my heartbreak turned to fury. I kept thinking, "How can I help to find this person and make him pay for taking my friend away from me? How cruel could he be for not even stopping to take my friend to the hospital? He must pay for what he's done." This was the defining moment for me that solidified what I would aspire to in life. Losing my friend inspired me to pursue a career in law. I made a promise to myself that I would one day find this man who killed my friend, and I would be the lawyer on the other side of the stand asking the judge to give him life in prison.

Whether you are driven by tragedy like I was, inspired by positive people and experiences, or motivated by a problem you want to solve, I'm sure you have dreams and aspirations. You may have just one definitive dream or a list of things you aspire to. Your dream may be as simple as thought or an idea. It could be something you always wanted to do but have never been able to start or complete. Your dream might even be a prophetic message or divine calling. Whatever the case, you cannot expect to fulfill your dreams until you first acknowledge what they are.

It's important for you to take some time to reflect on these dreams and the moments that brought you to them. Look back on your life and identify those things that made you want to be and do better.

WRITE IT DOWN, MAKE IT REAL

But don't just keep it in your head. You have to lock in on your dreams and make it real by writing it down.

"Write the vision and make it plain on tablets, that he may run who reads it." Habakkuk 2:2

Putting your dreams on paper also allows you to see them every day, etching them into your mind and serving as a constant reminder of what you want for your life. But there's also a scientific reason why you should take the time to jot your dreams down. A study by Dr. Gail Matthews, a psychology professor at California's Dominican University, found that when you write your dreams down regularly, you are 42% more likely to achieve them. This is because thinking about your dreams taps into the imaginative right hemisphere of your brain but writing them down brings in the logical left hemisphere. This shift is very important because you begin the process that moves you from imagination to action.

Back in the third grade, I wrote my dream of becoming a lawyer and living in California by the beach in my diary. I knew, even then, that it was important for me to put my goals on paper. The diary was nothing fancy, just a simple little hardcover notebook that I used to write my plans down. The power isn't in the style of the book—you can use a leather-bound notebook or a piece of scrap paper—or even the eloquence of the words you use, but in committing to your dream by getting it out of your head and down on paper.

INVITE GOD TO THE TABLE

Now that your dreams are in writing, spend some time with God. Speak with Him and ask Him to help you identify what His dreams are for your life. Before you start making plans, you want to first be sure that the dreams you have for yourself are aligned with God's purpose for your life. Otherwise, you will find yourself confused, lacking focus, and spending time and money pursuing an empty dream only to turn up empty-handed and disappointed, or you will find yourself accomplishing your dream but feeling unfulfilled.

I'll give you an example. One of my clients once told me that he spent all his life wishing to be a stock broker. He saw that stock brokers drove fancy cars, had beautiful homes, travelled the world, ate well, and had upbeat social lives. His dream was motivated by his desire to share in that lifestyle. So, he pursued a career as a stock broker, but when he finally got to that point where he had it all, his life still felt empty. He felt unmotivated and could not keep friends in his industry because conversations with them lacked substance. He knew there was more to life than what he had bought into.

As Rick Warren puts it in A Purpose Driven Life, knowing your purpose focuses your life, gives your life meaning, and motivates you. [1]Knowing this and understanding what our life's purpose is will allow us to live fuller lives and have deeper connections with others.

Do be mindful that God always has a bigger and better purpose for our lives, and His plan or dream for our lives will always prevail. Learn to ask Him to place visions and dreams inside of you that are in alignment with His will for you. And then trust Him and listen when He answers.

"Many are the plans in the mind of a man,
but it is the purpose of the LORD that will stand."
Proverbs 19:21

Learning to discern God's plan for you is essential. I can remember a few times in my life where I thought my plans for myself were the plans that God had for me. I soon found out it was not so.

For example, when I had my third child, I was in a wonderful relationship and was looking forward to getting married. I had rejected a proposal from my fiancé once before, but when he proposed a second time, I thought it was a sign that we were meant to be together forever. I was a mother of three but had never been married, and I thought I finally had a chance to do things the "right" way and raise my children in a happy two-parent home. So, I accepted the proposal.

I found myself the most beautiful dress I'd ever laid my eyes on. The reception venue and church were booked and holding fees were paid. I hired a wedding planner and had everything in place. We spent loads of money getting our wedding planned. But there was a small voice inside of me saying this was not God's will for my life. I tried to ignore the voice, but my stomach just didn't feel right about the wedding. Something was off.

1 Warren, Rick. Pg.34-36

Surely enough, one night I went home and asked my fiancé if he was excited about marrying me and starting our future together. He turned to me and said, "T (my nickname), I don't want to marry you. I am not ready to get married. I don't want to get married until I'm in my forties." I was devastated! I was in my mid-thirties and had been dating him for over seven years.

I contemplated whether I should wait until I turned forty for him to marry me. But I started to process everything in my mind and looked back at previous conversations. I thought especially about the way I felt when I decided to accept the proposal. I realized all along that the little voice inside of me was the Holy Spirit trying to tell me that this was not God's will for my life. His will was not for me to marry my fiancé.

I know for a fact that, had I married my fiancé, I would not have had the opportunity to fulfill my dreams and motivate and inspire so many women. My life now is far better than what it was then. I enjoy my philanthropy work in the community, being a leader in my business, and a spiritual mother to so many.

This is why you must ask God to show you His purpose for your life, direct your path, and give you wisdom, knowledge, and understanding so you may be able to understand His voice and be wise enough to walk into your destiny. Ask Him to use your life for His glory. Believe me, He will answer you. You will soon realize that you have a clearer understanding, focus, direction and the wisdom to know how to get there. Your dreams will not only come true, but they will be in alignment with God's purpose for you.

Be patient in this process. The answers may not come to you the very first time you sit with the Lord. It may take a little time for things to become very clear. The most important thing while you are going through this process is to allow yourself to explore, ask questions, meditate and write your thoughts and answers down. In time, the vision will become clear.

Also, understand that this is an ongoing process, even as you become certain of your dreams and God's plan for you. I myself continue to go through it. It has become a way of life for me. I never make a decision in my life without first taking some time alone with the Lord—speaking to Him, meditating on His Word, and writing my thoughts down. This helps me to always make the next best move. Make this a regular practice. Not only will it help you make the next best move, but it will also help you to lock in on your dreams and gain clarity, focus and confidence in your decisions.

FROM DREAMS TO PLANS

As you seek God's counsel to determine the next best move towards your goals, you will need to make careful plans to bring those dreams to life. I understand that you might feel hesitant about making plans. You're not alone. I have had people say to me before, "Victoria, I don't make plans because one can never be certain what tomorrow brings." While it is true that we cannot know the future, and that all is in God's control, this is not an excuse to avoid planning.

"If it is the Lord's will, we will live and do this or that."
James 4:15

When speaking to the people travelling with him about the cost of being a disciple, Jesus explains to the crowd how essential planning is. "Suppose one of you wants to build a tower. Won't you first sit down and estimate the cost to see if you have enough money to complete it…Or suppose a king is about to go to war against another king. Won't he sit down and consider whether he is able with ten thousand men to oppose the one coming against him with twenty thousand?" (Luke 4:28, 31). Much like the builder and the king need to plan, so do you. Because without planning towards your dream, you cannot bring them to fruition.

So, just as you took your dream to God, and asked Him to guide you and align your vision with His purpose, you must also draw close to Him as you make your plans and trust that He will lead you in the right direction. This means that when your plans seem to be failing, you should seek Him and allow Him to correct your course.

I'll give you an example. When I became pregnant with my third son, I was attending law school in England. The pregnancy was not a part of my plan, and I was surprised to find out I was expecting. Nevertheless, I pushed through as much as I could. However, I reached a point where I just couldn't manage being away from home, and I returned to Canada to be with my family. I tried to complete my program after I gave birth, but for a number of reasons, it just wasn't happening. I was taking care of family, living with my fiancé at the time, and had three boys to take care of. I started to think that I should give up on my dream of becoming a lawyer. I started to doubt my abilities and capabilities. The plan I had laid out was failing, and I feared that my dream was not to be after all.

However, something inside of me—I guess you can call it my soul—was just not alive. I was losing sight of the dreams I had for myself as a child. I was getting further away from the opportunities a career in law would give me to serve and help others and fulfill the promise I made to my childhood friend. I was heartbroken at the thought of not providing for my family, falling short of my potential, and disappointing God. I knew I could not abandon the purpose God gave to me just because life was not moving in the way I had expected. So, I went to God in prayer, and then I adjusted my plan and approached it from a different perspective than I did before I had my children and became engaged. And because I trusted God to order my steps when my first plan failed, I earned my law degree.

So, though you cannot predict your future and you may have to change your plans to fit life's curves, never abandon your dream. Trust that the Lord will guide and direct you so long as your plans are in alignment with His will and His Word.

REFLECTION MOMENT

Complete the exercise below to help you identify and visualize your dreams and get you in the habit of writing your dreams down.

1. What are some of your dreams?

____

____

____

____

____

____

2. Think of the events or moments that have shaped your dreams. Write them down here.

____

____

____

____

____

3. Where do you see yourself in the next 5 years?

____

____

____

____

____

____

4. What steps have you taken towards your dream?

____

____

____

____

____

____

5. Does your plan align with God's purpose for your life?

Chapter Two:
THE DREAM FORMULA

Our dreams are sacred and the desire to protect them is natural. Sometimes we fear that others might judge our dreams or doubt our ability to make them come true, so we bury them deep inside of us and hide them away from the rest of the world.

But when your dream is truly your purpose, trying to hide it is futile. It's like a pregnant woman trying to hide her pregnancy. No matter how much she covers herself with layers of clothing, trying to hide her growing belly, she will have to give birth eventually, or she and the child will both die. Once she accepts that she must bring her child into the world, she learns to nurture it, love it, and become dedicated to it as it grows, regardless of how others might judge her.

The same is true of the dream that you wrap up and hide away inside of you. When you are afraid to dream big and share your ideas and passions with the world, you put both yourself and your dream at risk. By hiding your dreams, you miss opportunities to connect with people who are able to help you manifest them. And the longer you keep hiding and dismissing your ideas and visions, the more something inside of you becomes saddened, dismayed, and frustrated. You have to find a way to manifest your dreams, or else, like the pregnant mother, you run the risk of dying full of visions you never birthed.

FAITH IS THE KEY

I know that sometimes your dream may seem unattainable. Doubt might convince you that there is no way possible of accomplishing your vision and leave you feeling uncertain how to act on your dream. But don't let fear get in your way of being great. It is the enemy's job to keep us in a place of lack, a place where you feel you are incapable. But that's not the truth. If you've locked your dreams deep inside your heart, it's time to release those ideas, visions, and passions into the world by turning the invisible key of faith.

Adjust your mindset and believe that God would not give you an idea, vision, or purpose without giving you the ability to fulfill it. If He places something inside of you, He will equip you with the tools to manifest it. Remember the story of Daniel, Shadrach, Meshach, and Abednego who were called to train in the king's service. As faithful servants of God, they were determined not to defile their bodies with the royal food and wine and asked the guard for vegetables and water instead. God saw their faith and rewarded their commitment. "To these four young men God gave knowledge and understanding of all kinds of literature and learning. And Daniel could understand visions and dreams of all kinds" (Daniel 1:17). God gave them all that they needed to fulfill their purpose, and if you trust in Him, He will do the same for you.

Never shrink away from your potential and the greatness that is in you because it feels too big. Lean on faith because what seems out of reach for us is never too big for God. Think of David, who was only a shepherd when he slayed the giant, Goliath, with nothing more than a stone. Before David stepped to him with his slingshot, Goliath had terrorized Saul and his army. But David, just a young boy, trusted that God would help him defeat the Philistine warrior. "The Lord who rescued me from the paw of the lion and the paw of the bear will rescue me from the hand of this Philistine" (1 Samuel 17:37). No vision or challenge is too grand for God to handle, and God's vision for us is always bigger and better than what we imagine for ourselves. So, if your dreams are so big that they scare you, trust that God will help you conquer them.

FAITH WITHOUT DEEDS IS DEAD

Having faith in God's ability to help you accomplish your dream isn't enough on its own. As the Bible says in James 2:14, "What good is it, my brothers and sisters, if someone claims to have faith but has no deeds? Can such faith save them?" The answer is no. Having faith and not doing the necessary work to bring your dreams to life is just wishful thinking!

Faith allows you to trust that your dreams and visions will become a reality. But living and serving in your purpose requires you to do the work. Faith and work go hand in hand. Of course, there is no simple blueprint for achieving your goals, but there is a formula that should guide your steps:

FAITH ± WORK = A DREAM FULFILLED

Whatever you want to accomplish in your life, find out the necessary steps that you need to take to get you there. As I suggested in Chapter One, start by writing your dream down so you can make it tangible, see it clearly, and engage the part of your brain that deals in action. This doesn't just work for your biggest dreams, but for your day-to-day goals as well. For example, when I start my day with a task list, I'm more likely to complete all the items on my list by the end of the day. Seeing each task on paper motivates me to work towards my goal and helps me put a plan in action to get them done. This is also true for dreams. I went through my list and checked off what needed to get done at different stages throughout my journey. Use this strategy to get yourself moving on making your dreams happen.

Next, do your research. Look into the courses and trainings that can help you build the knowledge you need to achieve your dreams. Read books, watch videos, and attend lectures that can help you grow your knowledge. If you are unsure of what you need to get started, find a mentor who is doing the same thing that you want to do. Reach out to people you admire and ask if you could have a quick talk with them. Go to events attended by individuals with the industry knowledge you require. I can personally attest to the fact that being in the same spaces as people who are already doing what you aspire to is key to your success. As I was growing in my law career, I went to legal events and conferences for lawyers and law students. I also went to conferences and workshops for entrepreneurs and business managers. This helped me to make connections and develop professional relationships and mentorships.

You must match your vision with an action plan that will help you bring it to fruition. I'll give you an example of how I'm practicing that right this moment. I intend one day to run for mayor of my great city of Toronto. Here is what I've done so far to make that dream a reality:

1. I envisioned myself already a mayor. I picture myself shaking hands and mingling with politicians and Canada's elite. This keeps my dream on the forefront of my mind.
2. I wrote it down in my five-year plan. This holds me accountable to myself.

3. I did my research and sought out people in politics whose work I admire.
4. I go to the networking and social events that the politicians I admire attend.
5. I got a mentor in politics. At a networking event, I met a politician who agreed to mentor me.

This process is doable for everyone. When operating in your gifts and talents, things fall into place. But that doesn't mean it's easy. As I followed the process I describe above, I found it challenging because I am an introvert. I do not like to socialize and put myself out there in front of people I don't know because it burns my energy. However, I know it is necessary, so I pulled myself together and did it anyways. I confronted my fear of socializing and networking and did the work that my faith required. And because I continue to lean on my faith and push past my limits to do that work, I move closer to my dream of being a politician or Mayor of Toronto one day.

In the same way, you can push forward towards your dream. Envision yourself in the place you aspire to be, write it down and set a timeline for yourself. Take it to God in prayer and have faith that if your dream is blessed by God, it will be yours. And then do the work. Even if it's hard and even if it scares you. Just as I moved beyond my introverted nature to find a mentor and build my network in the political world, you can conquer the fears that might be limiting you from chasing your dreams. It is going to take persistence and great effort on your part. Sometimes it will be bigger and scarier than you imagined. There will definitely be times when the work feels too hard and the dream feels too far out of reach. But perseverance is key. If you remember that Faith + Work = Dream Fulfilled, you will persist through those challenges. Often, the difference between people who fail and people who succeed isn't luck, talent, or opportunities; it's the willingness to persevere and keep doing what needs to be done, even when things get hard. So, do the work, have faith, and be strategic, and watch your dreams manifest.

BE FIRED UP FOR YOUR DREAM

There is another essential quality you will need if you want to achieve your dreams: passion. Especially when your goals seem far out of reach, being passionate will help you to persevere. There needs to be a fire in your heart that drives you towards your dream even when everything is telling you it is impossible.

You may be asking, "Okay Victoria, so how do I do this? How do I remain passionate? What if there isn't anything that I'm passionate about?" You keep ignited by understanding that when you live in the will of God, things will come together. His Word says, "For I know the plans I have for you…plans to prosper you and not to harm you, plans to give you a hope and a future" (Jeremiah 29:11). Therefore, as men and women of faith, if we believe that our dreams are in alignment with God's plan for us, we must believe Him when He says this and live on His Word and promise. As His children, this is our birthright.

With this kind of faith, envision the outcome of your goals and celebrate them daily, trusting that as you do the work God will deliver them for you. This is one part of the root of passion. The other part is gratitude. When you are faithful and grateful, you celebrate every single accomplishment that you make towards your dream or goal. You don't despise the small achievements for the bigger ones because you know small ones are just as important to getting you to success. Being able to recognize this helps to keep the fire of your passion for your reams burning brightly.

Of course, as challenges arise, and doubt springs up to block you, it can be easy for those fires to flicker. When this happens, take action. Spend some time doing things that relate to your dream and take some time to reflect on the achievements you've accomplished so far. Surround yourself with things and thoughts that remind you why you started in the first place. For example, completing my undergraduate program was very difficult, and I sometimes felt like time was at a standstill. To help me get through this period, I constantly reminded myself that I was accepted into one of the best schools in Canada. I recognized that I was very lucky because there were others who wanted to be where I was but did not get that chance. I also reminded myself that this was a necessary step if I wanted to write the California Bar Exam or the Canadian Bar Exam one day. So, I celebrated every exam I did and every result I received, whether the grade was high or not. I especially celebrated my winning moments because every little win meant that I was closer to my ultimate goal. This attitude kept my passion ignited.

Whatever your aspirations, commit yourself to keeping the passion alive. Do not allow challenges on your path to out your fire. Spend time reflecting on your journey and how far you've come. Celebrate all your victories, however big or small, and remember how you felt in the moments when you achieved them. Remember the things that sparked your desire to pursue the dream in the first place and keep them at the front of your mind.

REFLECTION MOMENT

Complete the following exercises to help you unlock your dreams and discover your potential:

1. What fears are keeping you from pursuing your dreams?

____

____

____

____

____

____

2. What are five things you can do today to help you start moving towards your dream?

____

____

____

____

____

____

3. To make sure the fire of your passion is not extinguished, it's wise to have a plan in place for when the flames start to flicker. List three things you can do when you feel your passion start to waver.

____

____

____

____

____

____

____

____

____

____

____

____

____

Chapter Three:
STAY FOCUSED

In today's social media world, it is so easy to get distracted. From Facebook and Twitter to Instagram and Snapchat, we are constantly bombarded with people posting and sharing their every move, meal, and moment. They share even the most intimate details of their lives including their income and romantic relationships. If you're not careful, you can waste your entire day scrolling through the "best" version of people's lives on social media.

The American Journal of Medicine recently found that 89% of young people use social media and are spending on average of nine hours on social media daily over multiple platforms. That's almost 40% of their day! This is concerning as research has shown that overuse of social media can have negative impacts on a person's mental health including depression, envy, decreased self-esteem, and risky behaviours. [1]This is especially true for people still in the process of determining their own path.

As a youth mentor, I've had many conversations with young people who have expressed that they're clear and focused on their dreams and goals until they open their Facebook and Instagram and see others achieving and celebrating their accomplishments. Suddenly, they begin comparing themselves and fall into doubt and feelings of inadequacy. This then leads them to re-think their dreams and want to chase other people's passions.

---

1 Journal of Adolescent Health, Volume 60, Issue 2, Supplement 1, Pages S75–S76

And it's not just young people. I've experienced this myself. I once took an online boot camp with Patrice Washington that I hoped would teach me to use my talents and gifts to create an income. I already knew what my gifts and talents were. I knew I also wanted to create a business that I was passionate about. The boot-camp helped me to identify my skills and my sweet spot. And then I opened my social media and scrolled past a post about someone's business that immediately sparked my envy. That person was putting themselves out there and was making moves— moves I thought I should be able to make. In fact, I thought I was even more educated and was in a better place than that individual to do what they were doing. Despite just having completed a boot camp to help me confirm my calling, and despite knowing the gifts God gave me, I chose to follow that person's business model and concept. It was only when I attempted to create the same business and copy the same model that I realized it was not an area that I was passionate about. My goals were not their goals, my dreams were not their dreams. There was no fulfillment for me in what they were doing.

There's a reason they say that comparison is the thief of joy. Comparison will drive you to a mental institution! Don't give into it. Remember that you are unique. God has a special purpose for your life that only you can fulfill. Your greatness and potential can never ever be unlocked or fulfilled by anyone else except for you, and you cannot unlock anyone else's. I've come to realize that no matter what others are doing, I have to keep my eyes on my prize and my gifts. I love using my prophetic abilities to teach, share love, and be of service to others. Those are the things I need to stay focused on.

So, guard your heart and mind. While social media can be a helpful outlet for self-expression, branding, and building connections, don't allow it to distract or discourage you from completing your goals and fulfilling your dreams. Create boundaries and limit your usage. I understand that social media can often feel like a break from reality, but we must remain cautious that we are not persuaded by other people's social media activities. Above all else, you must come to a place where you are happy and confident in your own abilities and capabilities. Believe in your dreams because you first need to believe in them before others will believe in you.

"Let your eyes look directly forward, and your gaze be straight before you." Proverbs 4:25

THE ULTIMATE MOTIVATOR

Remember the story that I shared with you earlier about my client, the one who wanted to be a stockbroker but was feeling unmotivated? It was only when he stopped wanting to be someone else and embraced his unique calling, gifts, and talents that he became excited about life. You see, my client became unmotivated because he wasn't living his life's purpose. His dream was shaped by what he perceived was happiness. His vision was not aligned to his true purpose.

Do your dreams excite you? Are they so big and so passion-filled that they scare you a little? If your dream doesn't make you want to spend all your time researching about it or trying to figure out how to make it come together, maybe you're in the same place as my client and it's time to re-evaluate it. Perhaps you need to press pause and assess whether you're doing what God called you to do.

The funny thing about callings is that sometimes we're not sure whether we should answer. I once heard the Holy Spirit speak to me and tell me I should accept an offer from the University of Southern California. I thought I was having some kind of odd experience. I hadn't submitted an application to USC, and I didn't know if I should have. USC is very expensive, and at the time, I had 3 children to care for. A Master's degree at a prestigious school cost over 60,000 USD—way out of my budget. However, after browsing their website, reading reviews and visiting the campus, I became excited about the thought of attending. And that's when it clicked. My excitement kept me motivated. Though I still had no idea how I would pay the tuition fees, I trusted that the Lord would not lead me astray. Trusting in his promises and faithfulness, I submitted my application to USC. Two months later, I was accepted. Going to USC fulfilled a dream I'd always had—to live in California.

That's the power of motivation. Along with your passion and the things your heart desires, it will give you the courage to take steps to achieve your dreams. However, I understand that this can be difficult for some people. It's why so many of us turn to external sources like music, videos, motivational speakers, family, or friends to stay motivated. There's no harm in that, but it's important to remember that lasting motivation comes from God's Word that dwells within us. [2]This means that He has given us everything we need to keep us going. We just need to activate the greatness and the power that's within us by allowing the Word of God to fill us up and listening when He speaks.

When lack of motivation creeps in, I remind myself that God promises to give us wisdom where we lack, to catch us where we fall, to never leave us nor forsake us. [3]So when I find my excitement and motivation faltering, I look to Him. I meditate on His

2 1 Corinthians 3:16

3 Deuteronomy 31:8, James 1:5

words to activate my power within.

"He gives strength to the weary and increases the power of the weak." Isaiah 40:29

With His words, you will build upon your faith in Him and discover new motivation from within. You will find that you no longer need to wait for Sunday service or turn to others to feel excited about your life. Trust me when I say His Word is enough. Mediate on his words daily. Tell Him when you feel weak and unmotivated. When you let Him know that you are faltering, He will remind you of your purpose and renew your excitement and motivation.

While you're putting your faith in God's ability to keep you motivated, be careful of people who lean on your energy and motivation to prop themselves up. Oprah Winfrey calls them "human energy vacuums" who suck the daylight out of you. You share your dreams with them and all of a sudden you lose motivation. Be wary and cautious not to surround yourself with people like this. Instead, continue to build your spiritual relationship with the Lord and let Him keep you full and on track to your dreams.

GET OUT OF YOUR OWN WAY

No matter how well you've planned, you won't reach your goals if your mindset isn't right. Why? Because if your mind is focused on everything but what you really want, you'll never achieve it.

Far too many people live and die with their dreams unfulfilled because their mindsets stunted their progress. I never wanted that to be my story. But avoiding that fate meant changing the way I thought about myself, my goals, my desires, and the life I wanted.

I needed to condition my mind to let go of the life I'd grown accustomed to. I had to train my mind to turn away from the lives I saw my friends living.

I grew up in Montreal surrounded by people who had limited mindsets. All of my friends were teen mothers who chose to get pregnant because they wanted to escape their parents. Many of them had two or three children, lived in public housing, and depended on welfare checks to get by. To them, that was freedom because their mindsets were limited.

Though I knew I had an entrepreneurial and professional mind, I fell into their ways of thinking. I became promiscuous, searching for someone I could have a child with, so I could be free from my abusive mother. Just like my peers, I struggled to imagine another way of experiencing freedom. Fortunately for me, there was something deep inside of me that told me this was not the only way. I knew I was meant for more than that. And so are you.

Even when your environment presents challenges, and you struggle to separate yourself from the way your friends and family think, I implore you to choose a different way. Dedicate yourself to shifting your mind away from limiting desires and attitudes and towards a godly and empowered mindset.

Here are a few things you can practice to help you condition your heart and mind to follow God's purpose and achieve your dreams for your life regardless of your circumstances:

» Get into the habit of speaking positivity into your life every

day.

The language you use to describe yourself and your life will have an impact on how you navigate the world. If you always speak about your life in terms of what you lack or how you're struggling, you will have a hard time seeing yourself in any other way. Learn to acknowledge the good that is already in your life, and faithfully believe that the things you desire will become yours. Begin every day with a prayer of gratitude, thanking God for all the good He has already done for you. Then, practice affirmations that remind you that your potential is beyond your current circumstances because there is nothing God cannot do. Whenever you are tempted to doubt yourself, try saying, "I am a child of God, and through Him, all things are possible."

» Remind yourself of your goals and your dreams.

Do not allow your environment to make you forget or abandon your dreams. I told you earlier to write your dreams down, because that will help to etch them into your mind. I encourage you to write them somewhere that you will see them every single day. Create a vision board or write your goals on sticky notes and leave them around your room. Use them as the background photo on your phone and computer. Write them down every morning in your journal. The more you think about and envision your dream, the easier it is for you to make it your focus.

» Turn to God's words and read his assurances that He has a plan for your life.

God's Word is full of messages and reassurances that he has an amazing plan for your life. Hold those scriptures near and dear to your heart. When you feel like you cannot move beyond your circumstances, re-read Jeremiah 29:11 and be reminded that God's plan is to prosper you, and give you a hope and future. When you are afraid that you are not good enough, remember Philippians 4:13 says that you can do all things through Christ because He strengthens you. When you are being pulled away from God's Word and direction, recall Romans 2:2 that encourages us not to be conformed to the world, but to allow his Word to renew and transform your mind.

» **Learn to see opportunities in every obstacle.**

When you go through challenges, do you see an obstacle you can't overcome or an opportunity to grow? If you're dealing with hard times, you have to train your mind to find the advantage. Remember, God uses difficult circumstances to build you up and make you stronger, strong enough to pursue your dreams. James 1:2-4 tells us to be grateful for all our experiences, good and bad, because those tests help us to become steadfast and steadfastness helps us to become whole and complete.

Above all else, always lean on faith. When you build on your faith, you adopt a mindset of prosperity. That is where you need to have your thoughts at all times. Get into the practice of believing God's words and the promises that He has made to you. Your mind will be at peace and the way you think about your future will be positive. You will trade anxiety for comfort and doubt for confidence. Accept and believe that you were made for greatness, and your destiny awaits.

REFLECTION MOMENT

Complete the following exercises to help you stay focused on your dreams.

1. Have you ever encountered a time where you wanted to give up on your dreams? If so, what were your reasons? What did that experience teach you? How did it make you feel?

____

____

____

____

____

____

____

____

____

____

____

2. List 3-5 ways you keep motivated.

____

____

____

____

____

____

3. How do you feel when you read and meditate upon God's words?

____

____

____

____

____

4. Remind yourself of your goals and dreams. Write them out below.

____

____

____

____

____

____

____

5. Write 3 special things about yourself that you have never shared with anyone.

____

____

____

____

____

____

6. What are you thankful for?

____

____

____

____

____

____

7. What is your current mindset?

____

____

____

____

____

____

8. Use this space to create your strategy for shifting your mind-set. Write down your favourite scripture and affirmations and the things you're most thankful to God for.

____

____

____

____

____

____

____

____

____

____

____

____

Chapter 4:
GUARD YOUR HEART AND YOUR DREAMS

When we have something beautiful in our lives, we naturally want to share. We do it all the time. The moment we receive good news—job promotions, pregnancy announcements, engagement stories, business launches—we call up the people we love or rush to our social media accounts to invite everyone to share in our excitement. I'm sure, that as you uncover the dream that God has placed inside your heart and become confident in it, it will fill you with the same kind of joy and the overwhelming urge to shout that news from the rooftops.

I encourage you to do this. A God-given dream is a beautiful thing, and every moment of the journey to achieving it should be celebrated. But, just as the Bible directs us to guard our hearts[1], it is important that we also learn to guard our dreams. Because not everyone will be eager to celebrate your dreams with you. There will be doubters and dream killers who try to fill your heart with fear and project their limitations on to you.

I experienced this often along my journey. In my high school years, when I told my family and friends that I wanted to become a lawyer, many of them told me that I wouldn't make it. They said that my grades weren't good enough, that I wouldn't be accepted to any law schools. Everywhere I turned, there were people who tried to turn me away from my dreams. And sometimes, it was

---

1 Proverbs 4:23

hard not to believe them because my circumstances often seemed dire and the path was hardly ever easy.

I had to lean hard on my faith in God and my certainty of his will for me to overcome the challenges that came up and the people in my life who didn't believe I could overcome them. I quit dancing and worked multiple jobs to make ends meet while I took care of my children and attended university. It took me many more years than most people, but I eventually completed my law degree at 39 years old.

If I had listened to everyone who questioned my vision or tried to pull me away from my dreams, I'm not sure where I would be today. I am grateful that God gave me the courage and the support to push back against the doubters and dream killers in my life.

You will need to do the same. Because the doubters and dream killers are inevitable and sometimes, they will be the people who you love the most. But you cannot allow that to turn you away from what God has destined for you. I want to share with you the lessons that helped me identify my dream killers, slay doubt, and trust in God's plan.

SPOT YOUR DREAM KILLERS

If you're going to protect your goals from dream killers, it will be important to know how to spot them when they come into your life. To do that, you'll need to pay careful attention to how people respond when you share your aspirations with them. Here are some of the common behaviours to look out for:

» Their response is laced with doubt.

When you share your dream, they ask questions like, "Are you sure?" Or they start outlining all the reasons why they think you can't make your dream come true. Rather than celebrating your ambition, they question why you're aiming so high.

» They show no interest in your dream.

They aren't excited when you share your dreams or when you accomplish any of your goals. When you speak, they never ask questions about your progress, and they seem uninterested when you bring it up in conversation.

» Their criticism is harsh and unconstructive.

When you discuss your plans with them, they are full of criticisms, but none of that critique is helpful. They are quick to shoot down your ideas but never offer any suggestions on how you could improve them.

They point out your shortcomings and remind you of your "limitations."

These people are quick to remind you of your challenging circumstances like your education level or your social background. They use these to convince you that your dreams are out of reach.

» They try to sell you on "better" options.

These people try to offer you alternatives that they feel will be better or easier for you rather than looking for ways to help you pursue the vision you've shared with them.

As you read those descriptions, did specific people come to mind? Those are the doubters and dream killers in your life. I understand that it might hurt to recognize people that you love and care about in those descriptions. It is difficult feeling that your loved ones are not supportive of your goals. But realize that these behaviours often have very little do with you. People who cast doubt on other people's aspirations are often projecting their own fears and limitations, battling insecurities of their own, or speaking from a space of jealousy. While you trust that God can give you anything you ask Him for, they see possibility from their own perspective.

THE ONE TRUE STAMP OF APPROVAL

Of course, when doubt comes from the people you most want to support you, it can weigh heavily on your heart. It is easy for their words and responses to infect you and shake your confidence and derail you from your dream. But regardless of how others may doubt your vision, God chose you. As much as you want to be validated by the people in your life, God's approval means much more.

"Am I now trying to win the approval of human beings, or of God? Or am I trying to please people. If I were still trying to please people, I would not be a servant of Christ."

Galatians 1:10

Joyce Meyers encourages us to break away from our need for other people's approval with this powerful reminder: "God is not surprised by your inabilities, your imperfections, or your faults. He has always known everything about you and He chose you on purpose for Himself. Once we understand how God sees us through Christ, we can refrain from being oversensitive to what people think about us and feeling bad about ourselves. We don't have to be addicted to their approval, because we already have God's approval.", [2]She's right. The one true stamp of approval comes from God, and His love and support are the ultimate validation.

Building and maintaining your faith in God's approval is always a work-in-progress, and there will be moments that you still feel like you want other people's validation. When that happens, think back to those affirmations and scriptures you listed as a part of your mindset shifting strategy in Chapter 3. When you feel yourself struggling to push through the doubt of those around you, read those scriptures and repeat those affirmations to yourself. Hold those words close to your heart and use them to combat the whispers of doubt when they come.

PROTECT YOUR DREAMS

It can be hard to know how to navigate your relationships with friends and family who aren't supportive of your dreams. Because you love them, you want to keep your relationship with them, but every time you talk to them about your ambitions, you end up feeling discouraged. Here's a secret: you don't have to share your dream with them. One of the things I found most helpful for my relationships with the dream killers in my life is learning how to compartmentalize.

What compartmentalizing looks like will depend on you and the relationships you're dealing with. In some cases, you might choose to avoid talking to certain people about your vision at all. If they ask questions, keep your answers honest, but vague. If you know

---

2 Joyce Meyer – "Breaking the Approval Addiction" published on Medium.com

that the conversation veers towards doubt and criticism every time your dreams are brought up, this is a good strategy. There are many other things you can talk about with a person like this, your vision just isn't one of them. And that's okay. With people who struggle with limited mindsets, you can share the results at the end but keep the planning to yourself. This way, their doubt and criticism won't be able to influence you as much, and your success can act as a testimony of God's work. These strategies have worked well for me and have allowed me to maintain relationships with people I love while also guarding my dreams and protecting my vision.

There are times when these methods might not be enough. Sometimes, the dream killers in your life can be aggressive in trying to steer you away from your purpose. You have to know what kind of doubt is too toxic for you to tolerate. When a friend or family member crosses that boundary, it might be wise to actively distance yourself from them. There are times when you have to decide to love a family member from afar or end a friendship. I'll give you an example. My sister is a body confidence coach and has built a successful business helping her clients learn to love and embrace their bodies. While many people have supported her business, she has a friend that has cut her down at every opportunity, harshly criticizing her and filling her mind with doubts. My sister loves her friend, but their relationship is doing her more harm than good. If you've got a similar story, I would offer you the same advice I gave my sister. Sometimes, you have to make the tough decision to cut people out of your life when the relationship threatens your purpose. The truth is that not everyone is meant to be with you at every part of your journey.

GET THE RIGHT PEOPLE IN YOUR CORNER

Just because you might have to step away from the dream killers in your life doesn't mean you have to go it alone. Not everybody is a dream killer. In fact, sharing your vision with the right people can help you grow your dream to its full potential. Whether it's a mentor, coach, consultant, or a collaborator, having the right people in your corner is very helpful. In fact, the Bible encourages us to seek support and advice. Proverbs 15:22 says, "Plans fail for lack of counsel, but with many advisers, they succeed." I've learned firsthand how important it is to have good advisers to guide me as I work towards my goals. Back in Chapter2, I mentioned my political aspirations and how I've found a mentor who can teach me about the process of becoming a politician. I have sisters in Christ who help me remain focused on my faith as I work toward my goals. Over my career, I've built a network of entrepreneurs, businesspeople, and lawyers who I can reach out to when I need advice or help. I've created a great system of support in place of the dream killers and doubters in my life.

You should also be building a network of support. Develop friendships with people who share your ambitions and are striving towards their purpose. Find mentors and advisers who are experienced and knowledgeable in the industry you're working in who can offer you support and direction. As you build these connections, pray for God to give a spirit of discernment. He will help you to find people who have no hidden agendas, but genuinely want to see you succeed.

Remember as you foster these new relationships that God's love and plan for you is still your validation. If mentors give you advice that tries to pull you away from your purpose or if their counsel seems laced with doubt, you don't have to follow it. Just as you don't need the validation of friends and family who try to discourage you, you don't need the validation of mentors either. You can value and respect their advice and still know that nothing can move God's will for your life.

REFLECTION MOMENT

Complete the following exercises to help you guard your heart and your dreams.

1. As you read Chapter 4, were you able to identify the doubters and dream killers in your life? Use this space to outline the strategy you will you use the next time they cast doubt on your vision.

____

____

____

____

____

____

____

____

____

____

2. Is there someone whose approval you have been feeling badly about not having? Take some time to talk with God and ask him to fill your heart with feelings of validation and affirmation, then meditate on the following scriptures:

- This is what the Lord says: 'Cursed is the one who trusts in man, who draws strength from mere flesh and whose heart turns away from the Lord." Jeremiah 17:5

- "Do not conform to the pattern of this world, but be transformed by the renewing of your mind. Then you will be able to test and approve what God's will is--his good and pleasing and perfect will." Romans 12:2

- "Take delight in the Lord and He will give you the desires of your heart."" Psalms 37:4

- "Set your minds on things above, not on earthly things." Colossians 3:2

3. What kind of people will you start seeking out to help you bring your vision to life? Create an action plan for developing those relationships. Make note of people you would like to reach out to, networking/industry events you'd like to attend, and things you'd like advice on.

____

____

____

____

____

____

____

____

____

____

____

____

PART II:

ALL SUCCESS IS AN UPHILL BATTLE

Chapter 5:
A DREAM DEFERRED

What happens to a dream deferred?

Does it dry up
like a raisin in the sun?
Or fester like a sore—
And then run?
Does it stink like rotten meat?
Or crust and sugar over—
like a syrupy sweet?

Maybe it just sags
like a heavy load.

Or maybe it explodes.

- Langston Hughes, Harlem.

Close your eyes and imagine for a moment what it would be like to come to the end of your life and realize that you never pursued your dreams. Imagine never accomplishing your vision because you were too afraid, too discouraged, or too overwhelmed by all the obstacles that cropped up in your way. How would your heart feel? Would your soul be satisfied? Would your spirit be fulfilled? Dreams deferred often result in disappointment.

Famous African American poet Langston Hughes compares it to a festering sore, the stench of rotten meat, a heavy load, an explosion. His sentiments are very similar to Solomon's who says, "Hope deferred makes the heart sick, but a longing fulfilled is a tree of life." [1]

Of course, I understand that sometimes your dreams might seem like they're out of reach. Obstacles will come up that will trip you up and make the journey hard. Difficult circumstances and challenges will knock you down and leave you tired and frustrated. You'll make mistakes that will take you off the path and leave you feeling lost and without direction. But I want you to know that even if you fall off the path, take a detour, or stumble and fall, that you should not give up on your dream. In fact, those detours and obstacles, however awful they might seem when you're going through them, are an important part of your journey.

I remember when I was 17, I was desperate to go to college. I knew that getting started on my post-secondary education was going to be important to fulfilling my dream of becoming a lawyer. But at the time, I was living on my own and working a dead-end job. My paychecks weren't enough to cover my rent and pay for tuition and books too. So, I went to my father and asked him for help. My father was unable to read or write and didn't have an education, so I thought he would be eager to help me have better opportunities than he did. But when I told him I needed money for school, he told me he didn't have it and he wouldn't be going out of his way to get it either. Heartbroken, I turned to an aunt who I knew was wealthy and had the financial means to help me. But again, the answer was no. She felt that my education was my parents' responsibility.

My only option was my mother. My relationship with my mom

---

1 Proverbs 13:12

was very complicated. Just two years after I was born, she moved from Jamaica to Canada. I was raised by my grandparents until I turned 13 and finally came to Canada to join my mother. I only lasted two years living with her before the environment became too toxic for me to stay in and I moved out on my own. Still, I loved my mother very deeply and I would have done almost anything to make her happy and hear her say "I love you." So, when I went to her and asked her for money for school, and she told me the only way I could get the money was to go "run road" with my stepfather, I reluctantly agreed.

My mother, stepfather, and I pulled up in front of Sears, and my stepfather handed me a gift card. As my mother sat beside him in the front seat of the car, he instructed me to go into the store and redeem the cash from the card. I did as he said, but as I wrapped up the transaction and walked away from the cashier, something in my gut stirred. At the time, I wasn't aware that the gift card I had just redeemed was stolen, but my spirit knew that something about what I'd just done was wrong. As the fear and panic rose in my heart, I began to run out of the store. I was near to the door when I felt a hand grip the back of my jacket and pull me back inside. I had been caught by security and they called the police. I was arrested and taken to the police station.

Frightened and upset, I called my mother and stepfather from the station, but they refused my call, and when I attempted to call again, they promptly hung up the phone. I was in shock. I was left to take care of the situation myself. I ended up with a criminal record and I still didn't have enough money to cover my tuition or buy my books. The path to getting my education seemed impossibly blocked. I felt defeated and ashamed. For years, guilt about what I'd done, shame about my naiveté, and anger at my mother kept me shackled.

But I refused to give up. I remember reading Isaiah 54:4 which says, "Do not fear, for you will not be put to shame." In that moment, I decided that I wasn't going to let that roadblock keep me from my dreams. I decided to change my story. I sold all my belongings, moved away from Montreal where I had been living at the time, and started over in a new place.

A few years later, everything seemed to be on track. I earned my undergraduate degree, had my first son, passed the Law School Application Test (LSAT), and got accepted into University of Connecticut. I was ready for the next leg of my journey when another hurdle arose in my path. It was the summer before I was due to start school, and I was excitedly preparing when I received a phone call telling me that my little brother had gotten into a devastating car accident. When we were younger, because my mother was away, I often took care of my baby brother, and we were inseparable, so when I got the news, I was terrified. Thankfully, he survived but was badly injured and his recovery was going to be a long one. So, at 26, I put my dreams on the shelf, deferred my acceptance to University of Connecticut, and prepared to take care of my brother.

Those two incidents—one caused by my own foolish mistake and the other completely beyond my control—could have both derailed me from my dream. There were definitely moments as I was dealing with each one where I asked myself if pursuing my dream was worth it. There were days when I thought that those roadblocks would never clear. Here's how I found my way back each time.

USE FAITH AS A COMPASS

No matter how far away you stray for your path or how many obstacles set you back, your faith in God can always guide you back. Matthew 17:20 tells us that if we have faith as small as a mustard seed, we can move mountains. Faith will also show you how to recover from failure, bounce back from mistakes, and navigate your challenges with grace.

"Now faith is confidence in what we hope for and assurance about what we do not see."

Hebrews 11:1

If you've found yourself off your path, try this exercise: envision yourself already accomplishing your goals. Picture what it would be like to have that amazing career, to start that business, to meet the person God has saved for you, to hold the baby you've always wanted in your arms. Whatever your dream is, imagine yourself already in that space. The path that will get you there may not be clear to you now, but this is what we call blind faith, the belief that God can give us what we cannot see.

With that faith in your heart, start making the decisions that will help you move towards your dream again. If shame and guilt over past mistakes are crippling your progress, forgive yourself as God forgives you. He did not call you to your purpose because you are perfect but because he believes you are worthy regardless of your imperfection. Despite my brush with the law in my youth, I have still been able to have a successful career as a lawyer and mentor. That is God's love at work, and He will love you and move you towards the greatness of your destiny in the same way. Honour His mercy by acknowledging the shortcomings that pulled you away from your dream, righting your steps, and recommitting to your purpose.

If setbacks have made you feel like you cannot fulfill your vision, never forget that God gave you that purpose and He will help you fulfill it. There's a lyric from gospel duo Mary Mary that says, "Nobody told me the road would be easy, but I don't believe He brought me this far to leave me." A difficult road doesn't mean that God has abandoned you and it certainly doesn't mean you should give up. Commune with God and reconnect with your passion.

THERE'S A REASON FOR EVERY DETOUR

Whether it's a bad decision or an unfortunate tragedy, it can feel like your detours are nothing but misfortune. It's not unfair to recognize that these experiences are challenging and painful. But it is important that we learn to reframe our struggles. Challenges are often used to teach us important lessons, prepare us for our purpose, and even pave the way for our destiny.

Think of the story of Joseph. He dreamt of his father and brothers bowing down to him, and when he told him of this dream, his brothers jealously sold him into slavery. In Egypt he became a steward to an Egyptian official, but when the official's wife tried to seduce Joseph, he ended up in jail. While he was in jail, he interpreted a dream for the Pharaoh's chief cupbearer, and when the Pharaoh had a confusing dream of his own a few years later, the cupbearer called on Joseph to interpret the dream. Impressed by Joseph's wisdom, the Pharaoh made Joseph his adviser. Many years later, when famine struck the lands and Joseph's brothers came to Egypt to purchase grain, they bowed before him, not even realizing who he was. [2]

Joseph's dream came to fruition, but not before he endured slavery and false imprisonment. But as terrible as those experiences must have been, it was those very things that put him in a place

---

2 Genesis 37-43

for that dream to become reality. Had his brothers not sold him, he would not have ended up in Egypt, and had the official's wife not falsely accused him, he would not have met the Pharaoh's cupbearer in jail. As you endure your trials, have faith that God is able to use any circumstance—good or bad. Those challenges you are facing may be the foundation for your success.

That is God's work. But there is work that we must do as well. When we are faced with difficult times, God calls us to have a heart that is open to learning because he uses our hard times to mold us and prepare us. James 1:2-4 tells us, "Consider it pure joy, my brothers and sisters, whenever you face trials of many kinds, because you know that the testing of your faith produces perseverance. Let perseverance finish its work so that you may be mature and complete, not lacking in anything." When I reflect on those stories I shared with you, I realized how much growth I gained because of those experiences. Being caught up in my mother and step-father's illegal activities taught me to be more discerning, to choose honest paths even if they are not easy, and to be persistent in the pursuit of my dreams. My brother's accident taught me about the Christ-like traits of compassion and selflessness, things I sometimes see my colleagues in law struggle to practice. My setbacks prepared me for my comeback.

Spend time reflecting on your experiences—good and bad. Practice reframing them as learning opportunities. Look for the lessons, the things meant to test your character and your faith. If you are having trouble, seek God and ask Him to show you. God will let you know what it is that He is trying to teach you or what He wants you to see. Just keep your heart open to Him.

CLEAR YOUR HURDLES

If you've ever watched an Olympian run a hurdle race, you'll see that they run swiftly towards the finish line, clearing every obstacle with confidence and grace. What we see is an amazing athlete who makes a very difficult activity look very easy. But they didn't wake up one day just knowing how to clear those hurdles so easily. It took years of practice and training for them to reach the Olympic stage. I'm sure if you asked them, they would tell you that not every run has been perfect. They would have tripped over and crashed into hurdles. They might have suffered injuries. They may have had practices and competition races that were awful. But they run anyway, and they leap over those hurdles time and time again.

And let us run with perseverance the race marked out for us, fixing our eyes on Jesus, the pioneer and perfecter of faith.
Hebrews 12:1-2

You may not be a world class athlete, but you are running a race towards your destiny, and you do have hurdles to clear. So, what does your training look like? While we all have unique callings and dream, there are some universal things we can all do to prepare ourselves to overcome our hurdles and run a good race:

» **Make God your coach**

In Isaiah 41:13, God tells us, "For I am the Lord your God who takes hold of your right hand says to you, do not fear, I will help you." Prayer and meditation on His Word will help you develop the resilience and wisdom to overcome the obstacles in your life.

» **Create your ideal conditions**

You cannot control everything that happens to you. There will be parts of your journey that will be rocky through no fault of your own. This is why it is important that you choose the best for yourself in the situations you can control. Surround yourself with a "team" of people who will uplift you when you struggle and push you forward when you are tempted to give up. Connect with people who are doing what you want to do and spend time learning from them.

» **Run one lap at a time**

Every small step contributes to the race in the long run. I like to make to do lists that outline my steps for the next 6 months, year, three years and five years. The race looks long, and the hurdles look high when you try to tackle it all at once. But breaking your goals down into manageable steps makes the journey a little bit easier.

» **Know yourself**

Good athletes know their bodies. They know their weaknesses and strengths. They know when they need to rest, when to push themselves harder, and what it takes for them to refuel. In the same way, you need to know your soul, heart and mind. Know what makes you falter, what empowers you, and where you need to grow. Spend time being present with yourself and make sure you give yourself what you need.

Whatever your struggles, know that your dream is still yours to claim. Do not let your dreams deferred rot, sag, and explode. Do not let lost hope make you heart sick. Remember to rely on faith to guide you through, find the lessons in your challenges, and prepare to run a good race. The obstacles will come, but they don't have to stop you.

REFLECTION MOMENT

Complete the following exercises:

1. Take some time to reflect on the obstacles you've faced in your journey so far. What are some of the lessons you've learned from them?

CHALLENGE	LESSONS

2. Is there shame or guilt you're carrying that's keeping you from moving forward with your dreams. Use this space to write a letter of forgiveness to yourself.

____

____

____

____

____

____

____

3. Short steps help you make big progress. Use the table below to create your 6 month, 1-year, 3-year, and 5-year to-do lists.

Timeline	Tasks *(What you need to do)*	Action plan *How you're going to do it)*
6 months		
1 year		
3 years		
5 years		

Chapter 6:
GOD'S PERFECT TIMING

Sometimes, as we're on our journey toward our dreams, it can feel like someone hit the brakes on our progress. No matter how much we plan, everything falls apart. No matter how hard we push, nothing seems to be happening. No matter how hard we pray, it feels like God keeps saying no. What do we do in these moments? Do we give up; get frustrated that everyone seems to be speeding by us towards their own success; grow angry with God for leaving our prayers unanswered? No, when you feel like your vision is taking too long, remember that your life and your purpose are not on your clock, but on God's, and His timing is always perfect. If you are in a season where you feel stuck, it does not necessarily mean that God is saying no, He is simply saying 'not yet."

Think about the story of Jesus' friend Lazarus. When Lazarus got sick, his sisters sent for Jesus who was preaching just a few miles away. They knew that Jesus had the power to heal their brother. But it took Jesus several days to get to Bethany, where Lazarus lived, and by the time he arrived, Lazarus was already dead and buried for four days. Many of the people who were there felt like Jesus had failed Lazarus and his family. They asked, "Could not he who opened the eyes of the blind man have kept this man from dying?" [1] As far as they were concerned, [2] Jesus was too late and cost a man his life. But Jesus knew that Lazarus was dead even

---

1 John 11:37
2 John 11:14-15

before he began his journey to Bethany. "Our friend Lazarus is dead" he told his disciples, "and for your sake, I am glad I was not there, so that you may believe." Jesus wasn't too late, he was right on time to work an incredible miracle that would bring many people to faith.

The story of Abraham and Sarah also shows God's perfect timing. God had promised Abraham that he would be the father of a great nation, but at 99, Abraham still didn't have any children. Now, none of us expect a 99-year-old man and his elderly wife to be able to conceive a child, and Abraham and Sarah definitely didn't believe it either. As a matter of fact, Abraham laughed and said, "Will a son be born to a man a hundred years old? Will Sarah bear a child at the age of ninety?" [3]But as impossible as God's promise seemed, and as long as He had Abraham and Sarah wait, God delivered on His promise.

In both those stories, the answer was never no. It was just not yet. It was God saying "Wait on me. Trust in my timing. Let me work." In an age of instant gratification, this can be especially hard to do. We're not used to having to wait for things. We've been conditioned to want things right away and we've been given the impression that we have the power to control that. There's an express option for just about everything—you can order fast food, or drive in the express lane, or order express shipping, or go to the express checkout line, or fast-track your degree. Waiting isn't something society encourages us to do anymore. But when we are pursuing the vision that God places on our hearts, we have to step out of that fast-paced express lane kind of thinking and remember that God's timing triumphs over all. This means we need to get really comfortable with the practice of patience.

---

3 Genesis 17:17

PATIENCE IS AN ACT OF FAITH

It takes real faith to be patient is situations like Abraham's where it feels like time is no longer on our side, or in situations like Mary and Martha's, Lazarus's sisters, where it feels like waiting is costing us too much. It's easy to get caught up in feeling like every second you wait takes you further away from your dream and the possibility of it ever being fulfilled. But James 5:7 tells us, "Be patient, then, brothers and sisters, until the Lord's coming. See how the farmer waits for the land to yield its valuable crop, patiently waiting for autumn and spring rains. You too, be patient and stand firm because the Lord's coming is near." If you are confident that you have done your due diligence in working for your vision, and trusting that God will keep His promise, then you know that your waiting will yield results.

We have to remember that God says He has a plan to prosper us and give us a hope and a future, [4]and God is not in the business of breaking promises. So, we have to trust that when He says He has our best interests at heart, that He will make it happen for us. The prayers and dreams we brought to Him, He will fulfill them. We cannot try to force His hand or make Him work on our timetables either. When we are impatient, we are saying that we believe we know better than God and that we can do more for ourselves than He can. When we are patient, we show him that we trust in Him and His timing.

Joel Osteen said it very well, "Sometimes, when things don't happen on our timetable, it can be tempting to get discouraged. In the season of waiting, that's when you have to dig in your heels and refuse to give up! You have to know that God is doing something in you at the same time that he is doing something for you." Which leads to my next question...

4 Jeremiah 29:11

ARE YOU REALLY READY?

Sometimes the reason God asks us to wait is because we aren't ready to receive the blessing of our vision. I've spoken a lot about the lessons I've learned from my struggles and setbacks and how those moments prepared me to handle the new levels God took me to. All the times I had to wait to attend school, or had to prioritize my family over my career, or just flat out failed at things, those moments helped to me to grow and develop the character, skills, and experience I needed to be ready when I reached my goals.

The Lord is not slow in keeping his promise, as some understand slowness. Instead he is patient with you, not wanting anyone to perish..."

- 2 Peter 3:9

The first time I sat the LSAT exam, I completely failed. It was extremely discouraging. This failure came after my run-in with the law, my delayed undergrad, my stint as a burlesque dancer, and unexpected pregnancies. I had gone through so much and worked so hard to get to that point and failing that exam felt like I had hit a wall and that every road was leading me to another no. But I decided to take the test again because I didn't want to give up on my dream. I studied harder. I didn't just memorize the information, I absorbed it, got really familiar with it, got to know it inside out. The second time I sat the test, I passed, easily. Failing that test forced me to press the brakes and really process the things I was learning. For a lawyer looking to use my career to change lives and fight for justice, I needed that. It was important that I wasn't just rushing towards the title of lawyer, but really committing to being the best person to fulfill my calling.

Being made to wait is a lot like being planted. All the time we wait and the things we experience in those waiting periods are like soil. Our impatience and anxiety can make us feel like we're buried instead of planted, but if we are able to shift our perspective, we begin to see that all of those seasons of waiting are giving us time to sprout and blossom. As TD Jakes describes it, "God is establishing patience, character, and concentration in the school of 'nothing seems to be happening.' Take the class and get the course credit; it's working for your good." See your seasons of waiting for what they really are: seasons of growing.

"Let us not become weary in doing good, for at the proper time, we will reap a harvest if we do not give up.
- Galatians 6:9

Sometimes the growth that's being fostered by our waiting is our faith. Remember those stories about Abraham and Lazarus? God's timing in those situations was intentionally designed to teach people involved to have deeper faith in him. Joyce Meyer makes reference to 1 Peter 5:6—which tells us to be humble before God and he will lift us up when the time is right—when she says, "God won't allow us to succeed at anything unless we're leaning and relying on him. But when we humble ourselves under the mighty hand of God, in due time, he will exalt us. 'Due time' is God's time, when God knows we're ready, not when we think we're ready. The sooner we understand and accept that, the sooner God can work his plan in our lives."[5]

And God is willing to wait with us while we get it together. Our periods of waiting aren't just about our patience with God's timing, but His patience with us as we grow into His plans and purpose. God is willing to wait for us to catch up to His plan for us, not just because He loves us, but because our purpose matters

---

5 Joyce Meyer, "When God's Timing is Taking Too Long" Joyce Meyer Ministries

in His bigger picture. 1 Corinthians 12:27 tells us that we are all the body of Christ and each of us has a part to play. God waits for us to grow and be ready so that we do our duties and fulfill our role as part of the body. This also means that sometimes we are waiting because our story and our path is tied to other people, and God is working on them too. We may never fully understand why God is asking us to wait because His wisdom is infinite, but as Proverbs 3:5-6 encourages us, "Trust in the Lord with all your heart and lean not on your own understanding; in all your ways submit to him, and he will make your paths straight."

KEEP YOUR EYES ON YOUR PRIZE

As you grow through your seasons of waiting, do not let yourself be distracted by other people's paths. Don't allow yourself to be discouraged when you see people enjoying seasons of success. Their path is not your path, and their story is not yours. Envying will not help you get closer to your dreams or speed up your process. It will take your eyes off your own path and pull you in directions that are not meant for you. You are also poisoning your heart with jealousy that makes it hard for you to hear God's calling and see the path He's laying out for you.

But we are human, and sometimes, especially when our season of waiting feels too long, jealousy will creep in. So how do you remedy that when it happens? Here are a few antidotes to envy:

- Remember that envy is a destructive emotion. Proverbs 14:30 says, "A heart at peace gives life to the body, but envy rots the bones." Being caught up in what other people have and being consumed by jealousy only causes you turmoil. Learn to identify envy and cut it out right away.

- Reflect on your progress to replace envy with gratitude. Whenever you are tempted to give into feelings of envy, spend some time thanking God for all of the things He's brought you through and blessings He's given to you already. Thank Him in advance for what He's going to give you because you know that He will keep his promises to fulfill your dreams. A heart filled with gratitude leaves very little room for envy.

- Remind yourself of your unique calling. Proverbs 4:25 tells us to keep our eyes forward and our gaze straight. Focusing on the purpose God placed on your heart is doing exactly that. If you are focused on fulfilling your purpose, you won't have time to be envious of what other people are accomplishing.

- See other people's success as proof of God's work. Witnessing other people's seasons of harvest as we experience our seasons of growth should remind us of how good God is and reassure us that he has greatness in store for us as well.

Always keep your eyes on your prize and on God. Don't let envy, doubt, or impatience take root in the soil that God has planted you in to grow you. Just like you pull weeds out of a garden to protect the plants, you have to weed out the negative things that can strangle your growth. Instead, nourish yourself with prayer and God's Word, do the work you need to do to help your growth, and trust that God will let you blossom when it's time.

REFLECTION MOMENT

Complete these exercises:

1. Take some time to reflect on your journey and consider what areas of growth you can develop. Think specifically on skills, attitudes, and connections you need to build to help you reach your goals and what practical steps you can take to acquire these things.

____

____

____

____

____

____

____

____

____

____

2. Fill out the chart below to create your envy antidote.

Five challenges God has brought me through	Five people whose success I will use as proof of God's work	Five scriptures I will turn to when envy creeps into my heart
1	1	1
2	2	2
3	3	3
4	4	4
5	5	5

Chapter 7:
SHEDDING SKIN

Is your past holding you back? In Chapter 5, I talked a little about the importance of forgiving yourself for your past mistakes. But I do realize that this can sometimes be harder than it sounds. The things from our past that we hold on to tend to bring heavy negative emotions with them like guilt, shame, fear, doubt, anger, and self-loathing. These are ugly feelings that dig their claws into our hearts and poison our souls. They feed the little voice in our heads that tells us that our dreams are impossible, that we are not worthy, and that we can never be more than the sum of our mistakes. But, when we don't address the burdens of our past with the same grace and forgiveness that God gives us, we keep ourselves from our full potential. We put limits on our ambitions, count ourselves out of opportunities, and close ourselves off from God's blessings.

YOUR PAST IS NOT YOUR FUTURE

If God forgives us, who are we to not forgive ourselves? I remember after my arrest in my teenage years, I felt terrible for putting myself in that position. I was terrified that people would judge me and see me as nothing more than a criminal. So, when job opportunities came up—jobs I desperately needed—I didn't take them because I was scared of having to explain my arrest record to interviewers. I felt like I was imprisoned by my past.

But as I grew to understand God's grace, I decided it was time to take steps to leave my past behind. With the assurance of God's forgiveness, I submitted my application for a governmental pardon which would clear my name of the crime I had committed. It wasn't about sweeping it under the rug. It was about letting go of the shame. Writing my California bar exam meant that I had to disclose a lot of personal information, including any history of crime or arrests, even things that were pardoned. Making peace with my past gave me the confidence to reveal my record without fearing that it would keep me from my dreams.

"But one thing I do: Forgetting what is behind and straining toward what is ahead, I press toward the goal to win the prize for which God has called me heavenward in Christ."
Philippians 3:13-14.

This is the promise of God's forgiveness and grace. 2 Corinthians 5:17 tells us, "If anyone is in Christ, the new creation has come. The old has gone, the new is here." Like a snake shedding skin, when we commit ourselves to God, we shed the mistakes and circumstances of our pasts. This means that they are just a part of our experience, not a definition of who we are. They don't determine what we're capable of or what we deserve. God wipes our slates clean and washes away all of our sins, and with it the shame, guilt, and fear.

We cannot sit around and mourn our pasts. There is no way we can undo our mistakes and regret is never going to help us move forward. Instead, we should do our best to right our wrongs, and commit with our whole hearts to being better than we were before as we press forward towards the dream God has given us. Just like we used the lessons we learned from the roadblocks and challenges we face in our lives, we can also take lessons from the errors of our past. Do not feel that those lessons are less valuable because of how you earned them. Learn to compartmentalize the mistakes from the lessons. It's like receiving an amazing gift in ugly wrapping paper. You wouldn't throw away the gift just because you don't like the packaging. The gift is still valuable and that's what you hold on to.

LAY DOWN YOUR BAGS

Sometimes, the things that haunt us from our past are not our own mistakes, but things that have happened to us. But just like our mistakes, being hurt or discouraged by bad experiences can make us feel fear, doubt and shame. It is important that we allow ourselves space to heal from these heartaches and traumas so that we can see the blessings God has in store for us.

A good friend of mine, Angella, shared a powerful story with me about how letting go of her past helped change her life. Angella's first marriage was to a man who was looking for immigration status. What began as her trying to help someone in need ended in physical, financial, and emotional abuse. The situation became so dire that she was forced to leave her husband, and she and her children ended up homeless. In this challenging time, she found a relationship with God and started going to church. That's when a sister in the church introduced her to a young man she thought would be a good match for her. But when Angella found out that this new man was also in the process of immigrating to Canada, alarm bells started ringing in her head. She worried that he would hurt her the same way her first husband had. But Angella turned to God for direction and the Spirit told her that this man was not like her ex-husband. She agreed to meet this new gentleman, and they have now been married for five years.

Angella's past experiences made her fearful, and understandably so. An abusive relationship is a horrible thing to endure and hard to recover from. This is true for most of the traumas and heartaches we face. Whether you've experienced domestic abuse, been neglected or abused by a parent, betrayed by a friend, or hurt by a stranger, these things bring complicated emotions. When these feelings go unaddressed and unhealed, they can get in the way of our destiny as we struggle to see beyond our pain.

"He heals the broken-hearted and binds up their wounds."
Psalms 147:3

Like Angella, when we are being held back by our heartaches, we need to pursue healing through God. In Isaiah 41:10, God tells us, "Fear not, for I am with you; be not dismayed, for I am your God. I will strengthen you, yes, I will help you, I will uphold you with my righteous right hand." God offers us healing for our souls. He invites us to lay down our burdens and relieve ourselves of the anxiety and heartaches that have been weighing us down. When we hand these things over to God, He gives a freedom where you can know that you are no longer a captive of your past. Know that no matter how terribly someone else might have treated you, God sees you as incredibly valuable and deserving of love. Choose to see yourself through His eyes rather than through the lens of those who have done you wrong.

LET GO WITHOUT FEAR

As you let go of guilt and trauma, you will find that you might also need to let go of other things in your life that don't align with your vision. Some of your old habits, behaviours and relationships will no longer feel like the right fit for you: the friends who encourage you to repeat bad behaviours; the relationships with family members who try to shame you out of your goals; the hobbies that don't serve your growth. You will need to shed all of the things that distract or discourage you from your purpose.

Of course, some things are harder to let go of than others. It can be scary to feel like we're losing things we need or cannot replace. But isn't that what faith is, taking a step even if you cannot see what comes next? When I first moved to Toronto from Montreal all those years ago, I had a son, no job, and no idea how I was going to survive. Like many women desperate to make ends meet, I became a burlesque entertainer. It was a very challenging time for me. I knew in my soul that it wasn't where I was supposed to be. I was sad and depressed. I looked into other job options, but with the best choice I found offering only $10 an hour, I knew that it wouldn't cover my mortgage. Even though everything in my heart was telling me to leave, I felt stuck.

It wasn't until I decided to trust God that I was able to break free. Stepping out on faith, I took a real estate course. It was a scary decision. I was moving into a new and unfamiliar industry where I had no guarantees that I would find clients or earn enough money. But I did it anyway. I got my license, bought a printer, made my own flyers and stuck them on people's doors. Then one day, I met a man in the mall with a real estate agency. Right there, he offered me an office space, and everything changed. Real estate wasn't my dream career, but it was one step closer. Had I let my fear keep me in the strip club, I don't know where I would be today.

Angella had a similar story. She also had children, but no secure way of providing for them, and she also found herself in the strip club. The money she made there paid for her rent and her tuition and allowed her to get off of welfare. But though she had the comforts of the world, her heart was uneasy. She felt like she was being disloyal to her grandmother who raised her and unfaithful to God. So, she prayed to God and asked Him to provide. She took her resume into Walmart and got a job cleaning at night. What she earned was a far cry from what she made dancing, but it was stable and helped her take care of her family. She eventually moved out of government housing and into a beautiful home of her own.

"Forget the former things; do not dwell on the past. See, I am doing a new thing! Now it springs up; do you not perceive it? I am making a way in the wilderness and streams in the wasteland."

Isaiah 43:18-19

What Angella and I did was not easy. It was terrifying to make the leap. But once we took that first scary step, God cleared the path and took care of our needs. Whether it's your job, your home, unhealthy relationships, poor lifestyle choices, or bad habits, when we let go of things that don't serve us, we make room in our life for much better things. Ridding your life of things that do not move you towards God's purpose for you is not a loss, it is a freedom. It's okay to feel fearful or nervous, but you have to push through it.

In his second letter to the church of Corinth, Paul writes, "We are troubled on every side, yet not distressed; we are perplexed, but not in despair; persecuted but not forsaken; cast down, but not destroyed." [1]Once you've shed the skin of your past and become who God calls you to be, you discover this perfect peace of

---

1 2 Corinthians 4:8-9

knowing that God can bring you through anything and make you new. Notice that Paul doesn't describe a life of perfect peace as easy or painless. He says that the church is troubled, perplexed, persecuted and cast down, but they are not broken by any of it. I cannot promise you that will never suffer or struggle. Satan goes after those who are living in righteousness. Remember Job? But with perfect peace, you will be confident that your struggles will not defeat you and that you are prepared to handle them because God is with you.

REFLECTION MOMENT

Complete these exercises:

1. What baggage from your past is weighing you down and keeping you from your purpose? As you write them down, meditate on giving them over to God.

____

____

____

____

____

____

____

____

____

____

____

2. Take a moment to reflect on your life. Are there toxic relationships, habits, or choices you're holding on to out of fear? Use the table below to identify how letting these things go will bring you freedom instead of loss.

WHAT ARE YOU HOLDING ON TO?	WHAT ARE YOU AFRAID OF LOSING?	HOW WILL YOU BE FREER WITHOUT IT?

3. Memorize this scripture and meditate on it whenever you are feeling trapped by your past:

"The Lord your God is with you, the Might Warrior who saves. He will take great delight in you; in his love he will no longer rebuke you but will rejoice over you with singing."

- Zephaniah 3:17

Chapter 8:
THE OTHER SIDE OF FEAR

There's a popular quote that says, "If your dreams don't scare you, they aren't big enough." I'm sure you've heard it before. If you've felt God's calling, then you know what that fear feels like. I do too. I've shared with you the many significant dreams God has placed in my heart: completing my law degree, pursuing a career in politics, building a loving family. At different stages of pursuing those dreams, I've felt some fear and anxiety about whether I could fulfill those dreams, whether I would fail, and how I would measure up to God's calling. Pushing through fears like these have always been a part of my process. But recently, I had fear grip my heart in a whole new way, and I knew that God had given me his greatest calling yet.

Not long ago, I was told by my spiritual life coach that God was calling me into Ministry. It wasn't the first time I had heard that. Both my pastor and church prophet had told me this in the past. But when my spiritual coach mentioned it to me, my heart filled up with hesitation. God couldn't possibly be calling me to minister. I am the perfect definition of an introvert. I am terrified of public speaking, I don't like to be the center of attention, and I am most comfortable alone. None of those qualities seemed fitting for someone called to ministry. How could God want me for this task? The more I thought about it, the more anxious I became. I didn't even want to entertain the idea.

Here's the thing about fear. It's a normal human emotion. Anytime we feel like we might be at risk in some way, fear comes in to warn us. Sometimes, that fear is based on real danger—standing at the edge of a cliff, walking down a dark alley, facing a violent situation. Sometimes, it's based on the discouraging whispers of doubt, anxiety, and anticipation of failure and discomfort. That kind of fear is the one that tends to cripple our dreams and makes us question or destinies. When our dreams are big and our goals seem impossible, that fear creeps in to tell us to quit, to run, to give up.

I felt all of that when I was told that God was calling me into ministry. But I've learned that when you're pursuing your purpose, that fear will come. I've also learned that it's what we do with that fear that matters the most. Do we persevere in in spite of it, or do we allow it to take hold and keep us stagnant? Do we get comfortable with what we know, or do we trust that God will get us to our destiny, no matter how unclear the path might seem?

I chose the latter. I am always reminded that fear is not from God. It is not what He asks us to do when he gives us our destinies. He asks us to have faith. As Charles Stanley puts it, "There are two paths you can walk: faith or fear. It's impossible to simultaneously trust God and not trust God." [1]I choose to trust God. I am always reminded that if God has called me to do greater things in life, then he will equip me for the job.

That reminder has encouraged me past my anxiety and carried me bravely through to my destiny. I faced my fears of ministry and answered God's call, and I am proud to say that I now lead a ministry called Sisters in Christ Empowerment Ministry. If I had trusted my fears, I would never have been here. But when I got out of my head and into God's Word, I was able to answer His call to

____

1 Crosswalk.com – Choosing Faith Over Fear

empower women, build them up, and help them walk in their own destinies.

I want the same thing for you. If anxiety and doubt are standing between you and your dreams, here are some of the important reminders that helped me cling to God and move through my fear.

FEAR: THE DREAM KILLER

Science tells us that fear triggers one of three responses: fight, flight, or freeze. When we are afraid, we will either resist the thing that frightened us, run away from it, or become immobilized and unable to act. If you're trying to pursue a dream that scares you, none of those reactions are going to be very helpful. When you give in to fear you forget to be courageous. Instead, you become stagnant, miss opportunities, and sacrifice your power and potential.

I'll give you an example. I had a friend named Lena. As a child, she loved swimming and had dreams of becoming a professional swimmer. One year, her father took Lena and her siblings to the beach. She was excited when he told her that he would teach her how to swim in the ocean. But during her lesson, something went wrong. Somehow, Lena slipped out of her father's arms and under the water. He caught her quickly, but by then, she'd already inhaled some water. She caught her breath after coughing up the water she had swallowed. The whole incident only took a few seconds, but it was enough to terrify her. She became so afraid of the water, she didn't swim again until she was a teenager.

When Lena and I became friends as teenagers, she shared her story with me, and I tried to encourage her to overcome her fear and pursue her dream of becoming a swimmer again. I convinced her to take swimming lessons with me. Still extremely anxious about the water, Lena panicked in the pool, and the water went into her lungs. That day, she gave up on her dream for good. The fear was simply too much. She gave it too much power, and it kept her from pursuing the thing she loved.

This is what fear does. If we don't check it, it kills our dreams. TV journalist Soledad O'Brien put it beautifully when she said, "I've learned that fear limits you and your vision. It serves as blinders to what may be just a few steps down the road for you." Fear distorts our vision. It tells us that we are not good enough, not strong enough, not smart enough, and not capable enough. It tells us that we are aiming too high and pushing too far and chasing things that we're not ready to do. That kind of fear can be very convincing, but it doesn't make it true.

AT THE ROOT OF IT ALL

So how do you fight fear? Dig in. Fears are like weeds. They dig in deep and take up space in the garden of your life. They choke out the things you really want to grow. If you want to conquer them, you have to remove them at the root. My first pregnancy was unexpected, but once I learned I was having a baby, I knew I wanted more than anything to be a good mother. Because of my experiences with my own mother, it was important to me to make sure that I was better for my children. But there was a lot I was afraid of. Everyone around me thought I had ruined my life. They didn't believe I would ever make anything of myself. They told me that I would never be able to achieve my dreams. My religious relatives told me I partied too much and lived too much in the world to be capable of being a good mother.

As a young pregnant woman, that stuck with me and struck fear into my heart. For a long time, I was afraid of failing as a mother and missing my purpose. For the first few years of my son's life,

I would take him to my mother's house so my grandmother could take care of him because I was convinced she would do a better job of raising him than I ever could. At one point, I even sent him to New York to live with my aunt because I trusted her to parent him more than I trusted myself. My anxiety about motherhood was that intense. I was a slave to my fear of failing as a mother.

It was not until I made the decision to be a good mother that I was able to overcome my anxieties. I wanted to have a relationship with my son and build a bond with him, and my fear was standing in the way of that. With prayer and determination, I made the choice to stop giving fear power over me. You see, fear does not have power on unless we allow it to. Our thoughts and our decision to believe them is what gives fear the ability to impact our lives.

Too often, we treat fear as if it were something precious adding value to our lives. But fear doesn't add anything to our lives. It stunts our progress, limits our growth, and makes our dreams seem impossible. But God tells us not to be fearful. 2 Timothy 1:7 says, "For the Spirit God gave us does not make us timid, but gives us power, love and self-discipline." If God gives us a Spirit of power, how can we allow fear to control our lives?

"Have I not commanded you? Be strong and courageous. Do not be afraid; do not be discouraged, for the Lord your God will be with you wherever you go."

— Joshua 1:9

Max Lucado compared fear to mosquitoes. He says, "Become a worry-slapper. Treat frets like mosquitoes. Do you procrastinate when a blood sucking bug lights on your skin? I'll take care of you in a moment'? Of course you don't! You give the critter the slap it deserves. Be equally decisive with anxiety." [2]When your fears

---

2 Maxlucado.com – A Worry Slapper

come up, sit with them right away. Explore where they come from and cut them out at the root. Confront your fears, make a conscious decision to change the way you think about the things that scare you. Decide that you will no longer allow them to have power over your life and consume your time. When doubt and anxiety try to deter you from following your goals, know that God's grace is sufficient, and He will guide you through everything you're afraid of on the journey to living your dreams.

DREAM BIGGER THAN FEAR

Fear is likely always going to be a part of your journey. As you push away fear to achieve one goal, it will crop up to deter you from another. Don't let that stop you from pushing forward anyway. Nelson Mandela once famously said, "I learned that courage was not the absence of fear, but the triumph over it. The brave man is not he who does not feel afraid, but he who conquers that fear." You're not courageous because you do not feel fear, you're brave because you have the faith to dream big and pursue those dreams in spite of the fear you feel.

As you get closer to accomplishing your dreams, the fear is likely to grow. Don't try to deny it. Acknowledge that fear, face it down, and get to the root of it. Ask yourself this question: Do I want this more than I am afraid of it? If your answer is yes, don't let fear make you shrink your dreams. If your answer is no, remember that God and his Word are the ultimate cure to fear. Fix your thoughts on Jesus and the promises he has made to us. He has assured us time and again that He would walk beside us, that He would not give us more than we could bear, and that He is more powerful than anything we could possibly be afraid of. Meditate on God's Word until your desire to walk in your destiny overshadows your fear of pursuing it. Trade your fear of failure, pain, and loss, for faith in God. Understand that on the opposite side of fear is an extraordinary life He has prepared for you.

REFLECTION MOMENT

1. Think about your goals. What fears have you been giving power to?

2. Reflect on your life and the things you've accomplished. What fears did you overcome and how can you use those experiences to put your current fears into perspective?

____

____

____

____

____

____

____

____

____

____

____

____

PART III:

LOOK HOW FAR YOU'VE COME

Chapter 9:
TO WHOM MUCH IS GIVEN

My story of success and destiny and all of the lessons I have shared in this book are a testament to God's grace and generosity. We serve a loving God who, though we have done nothing to earn it, showers us with blessings. When we are faithful to Him and trust his process, He guides our steps to a life full of purpose. From the breath in our lungs each morning to the dreams He places on our hearts, God is the perfect example of what it means to give with love.

No gift has been more precious that the decision God made to sacrifice his only son for our sins. He sent His son to earth where He was belittled, mistreated, and killed, so that we could have everlasting life. [1]As a mother, I recognize the magnitude of that sacrifice. And even after giving us such an incredible gift, He continues to give to us. God's generosity is as limitless as his love for us.

Now, we know that God calls us to be like Him and follow the example He has set for us. We also know that the Bible says, "From everyone who has been given much, much will be demanded; and from the one who has been entrusted with much, much more will be asked." [2]As God moves us closer to success and blesses us with the dreams and desires of our hearts, we are called to give back with pure and generous hearts.

---

1 John 3:16

2 Luke 12:48

"In everything I did, I showed you that by this kind of hard work we must help the weak, remembering the words the Lord Jesus himself said: 'It is more blessed to give than to receive.'"

– Acts 20:35

When we give back, we show that we appreciate what God has given us and that we heed His instruction to imitate Him. In my life, I've been fortunate enough to achieve many of my dreams through God's grace. I have a beautiful, loving family, I have earned my degree in law, and I have started a ministry for women. All of these things are blessings that God has entrusted me with. The very least that I can do is to give back to others. Whether that's financially through tithes or charitable donations, spiritually through fellowship and encouragement, or professionally through mentorship, it is important that I reflect what God has done in my life through acts of kindness and generosity of my own.

I recently spoke with a friend of mine and a member of my women's ministry, Tanasha, who reminded me how giving back not only humbles you and shows you where you've been and how far you've come, but allows you to contribute to God's kingdom and fulfilling His purpose in others. Something she said that really resonated with me was this: "Investing the value into someone else that God gave to you helps to build God's kingdom. Paying things forward helps us recognize the importance of loving each other as God loves us."

WHAT DO YOU HAVE TO GIVE?

Often, when people think of giving back, their first thought falls on financial giving. Of course, this is important. The Bible highlights the importance of giving our tithes [3] and taking care of the needy. [4] If you are in a position to make generous financial donations to the church, charitable causes, and individuals in need, you should. However, do not think that giving money is the only way God asks us to imitate His spirit of generosity.

As we step into our destiny and achieve success, we gain access to opportunities to uplift and encourage others around us with the gifts God has blessed us with. Romans 12:6-8 says:

> *"We have different gifts, according to the grace given each of us. If your gift is prophesying, then prophesy in accordance with your faith; if it is serving, then serve; if it is teaching, then teach; if it is to encourage, then give encouragement; if it is giving, then give generously; if it is to lead, do it diligently; if it is to show mercy, do it cheerfully."*

It is important then that we take time to examine our lives and the blessings God has bestowed upon us and determine how we can give back.

Personally, I have been given the gift of teaching, ministry, and encouragement. So, generosity for me has been about helping others by sharing my experiences and knowledge to empower them to overcome the barriers I once faced. I created a mentorship and leadership program specifically to help young people go after their business and career dreams because I know that was a gift God gave to me. I also started Sisters in Christ to use the gift of ministry to empower other women to build and strengthen their relationship with God. These endeavours have allowed me to show gratitude to God and all the people he placed in my life to pave the path that I followed.

---

3 Proverbs 21:13

4 Proverbs 19:17

Another important gift that we often forget is testimony. In 1 Peter 3:15, we are told to "always be prepared to give an answer to everyone who asks you to give the reason for the hope that you have." Our lives and our stories are proof of God's grace, mercy, and power, and can be a great source of encouragement for others who are feeling lost, hopeless, or doubtful. I think of someone like Oprah, one of the wealthiest women in the world, who has always been very financially generous, but has made her greatest impact because of her willingness to share her life. Before her success, Oprah endured a difficult childhood, a rocky career, and a number of challenges that would have discouraged the best of us. When she began to achieve her dreams, she did not hide her past away, but openly shared with millions of people all the hard lessons she's learned and the struggles she overcame to get to where she is. I know that I have been personally influenced by her ability to push past her circumstances and everything that tried to block her path. I look at her and I see a shining example of God's grace. That is the power of testimony.

NO TESTIMONY IS TOO SMALL OR TOO SHAMEFUL

I was having a conversation with some of the women in my ministry, and the subject of testimony came up. One of the things we talked about was the way that some Christians hide their testimonies away, unwilling to speak openly about what God had done in their lives. I've found that's usually because they are afraid of shame or insignificance.

If either of these thoughts is holding you in silence about the great work God has done in your life, here's what I want you to know:

THERE IS NO TESTIMONY TOO SHAMEFUL

If you are struggling with feeling ashamed of your past, I can relate. A few years ago, I would never have written this book. The idea of pouring out the dark details of my past so publicly was mortifying. I've shared candidly with you some of the experiences in my life and how for a very long time, they filled me with shame. I hid them because I was afraid of being judged by the high-class friends I had made during law school. I felt that some of them looked at me as an inspiration—"the Black girl who's doing well"—and I didn't want to reveal the truth about my past.

This feeling is not unusual. Two of my friends shared similar stories. Tanasha had been molested in her youth, and for many years, she carried that experience in silent shame. It haunted her dreams and made her deeply unhappy. When she started a job working at a high school, female students came to her to reveal their own experiences, but with her own pain unaddressed, she was unsure how to help them. Angella had also been sexually assaulted by a family member and became pregnant. She too felt deep shame about what happened to her, and she didn't know how to face the world or be a mother to her child.

All of us felt that our stories were too shameful to share publicly. Each of us worried about being judged for our pasts. But our pasts are not what defines us. When we gave our lives to Christ, we became new in him. In an article on the power of testimony, Joyce Meyer wrote, "I want to share my testimony because so many people have been hurt, and they need to realize that someone has made it through their struggles so they can have hope… That's why I'm telling my story. You need to know how good God is and that your struggle is worth it." [5] There is a lot of truth in that. Angella cites Joyce Meyer candidness about her own sexual abuse

5 Life Beyond Abuse" – Joycemeyers.org

as a part of how she came to see that God forgives and heals and we can move forward and tell our stories without shame or embarrassment. Tanasha found the same freedom. She told me, "I'm a different person today. So, when I tell my story, I feel good. If my story can help, why would I not share?"

Just like Joyce Meyer, Angella, Tanasha, and myself, you are not your past. You are not the terrible things that happened to you or the bad choices you made. You are a living testament to how powerful God's grace is and how He works to bring us through our darkest hours if we just have faith in Him. Do not let shame be a shroud that keeps you silent. When we share our pasts, no matter how ugly they might be, we help others see that they too can be saved and renewed by God.

THERE IS NO TESTIMONY TOO SMALL

Sometimes, we forget that even in our smallest challenges, God has our back. We think that the only testimonies that matter are the ones that are sensational and heart-wrenching. But it is the small moments of grace that can remind us that God never abandons us and none of our problems are too little for Him to love us through. When we share those stories, we encourage people to see that God's grace is limitless, His compassion for us is never-ending. He will never say, "I don't have time to help you with that" or "your problems aren't worth my attention."

Bree Joplin, a young woman who found her relationship with Christ at just seven years old shared that she used to feel that she felt her testimony wasn't important enough because it didn't have any drama. But here's what she realized:

"The truth is, every testimony is a story of dramatic redemption and unexpected rescue, no matter how mundane you or anyone else might view it. Sure, you may not have a testimony that makes the news or is put into some sort of motivational video, but that doesn't matter. Because of the sin that we are born into, any story of redemption is one worth telling." [6]

Do not ever feel that your testimony is too small. God has redeemed you just like he has redeemed someone with a dramatic and sensational story. Your story might be the one that someone needs to hear to remind them that no struggle or situation is insignificant in God's eyes. He loves us all and extends His grace to all of us as His children. Because of that, all of our stories matter, and all are worth sharing.

TO GOD BE THE GLORY

Something that we need to be mindful of when we give back, whether that's financially—through our gifts and knowledge, or through our testimonies—is that we are doing so with pure hearts intent on bringing glory to God. It is easy to give back for the wrong reasons. On one hand, generosity is often praised, and it is easy to get caught up in the validation that comes with that. But when we give back to make ourselves look good, we lose sight of the true meaning of charity and generosity. Giving, as I said before, is an act of gratitude and an imitation of God's love and grace. When we make it about ourselves, we forget that it is God who provided us with the ability and the resources to give back in the first place. 2 Corinthians 9:11 tells us that when we are generous, it will result in thanksgiving to God. When we center ourselves in generosity, we take for ourselves glory and praise that is not rightfully ours.

---

6 All Testimonies Matter. Including Yours" –The Odyssey

But when you give to the needy, do not let your left hand know what your right hand is doing, so that your giving may be in secret. Then your Father, who sees what is done in secret, will reward you.

- Matthew 6:3-4

We also must not give back with the expectation of getting something in return. Yes, the Bible tells us that God rewards those who give generously, but if we are imitating Christ, we have to remember that He did not make His sacrifice so He could demand anything from us in return. He gave us salvation purely because He loved us. There was nothing we did to earn it and there is nothing we can do to repay Him. In the same way, we shouldn't be generous with expectations of repayment, but because it is what God calls us to do.

So, when you give, do it with a pure heart that is focused on showing others how merciful and graceful God is. Do not brag or make announcements. Do not make the act of giving about the thing you have given. Remove yourself from the situation and focus on the kindness of helping others and the beauty of reflecting God's compassion.

"A generous person will prosper; whoever refreshes others will be refreshed" - Proverbs 11:25

Of course, I recognize that generosity is not always easy. Sacrifice is hard. We live in a society that encourages us to amass as much as we can and protect our own interests. Often, generosity can seem like you're risking more than you can stand to lose. If that doubt ever creeps into your heart, remember that God has never forsaken or abandoned us. Throw away that mindset of scarcity and trust that God will provide for you. There's no need to be fearful that if you give, you'll be in lack. God tells us that He loves a cheerful giver and He blesses the generous.

REFLECTION MOMENT

Foster a spirit of generosity with these exercises:

1. Re-read Romans 12:6-8. What are the gifts God has blessed you with? How can you use them to help others?

Gift	Ways I can use my gift for others

2. How can you use your testimony to bring glory to God?

____

____

____

____

____

3. If you're struggling to share your testimony because of fear of insignificance or fear of shame, meditate on the following scripture:

"Because of the service by which you have proved yourselves, others will praise God for the obedience that accompanies your confession of the gospel of Christ, and for your generosity in sharing with them and with everyone else."

– 2 Corinthians 9:13

Chapter 10:
FRIENDS IN HIGH PLACES

As you reach new levels of success through God's grace, you will encounter new challenges. One of the biggest ones for me was how to surround myself with the right people. Throughout my journey, there were many people in my life who I loved deeply, but they resented my success. I hoped that I would find love and support as I walked more and more in my purpose, but I sometimes found jealousy and bitterness instead. It was a difficult thing to deal with, and it often left me feeling very lonely. I also met new people who seemed to mean well, but their motives were not pure. But I learned that building an inner circle and support system was something I needed to be intentional about. I would need a network of people who would push me closer to God and my destiny rather than pull me away from it.

I have been very grateful to find that now. I have a loving family, a community of sisters in Christ, mentors who help me push toward my goals, and God, my greatest friend. That support has been vital for me and my success. As I sat down to write this chapter, I called up three of my closest friends, Angella, Stephanie, and Tanasha, (you may recall their names from earlier chapters) to talk about the value of support and sisterhood throughout our journey. These are women that I have shared my heart, my struggles, and my fears with. They've prayed for and with me, read scriptures with me, and helped me restore my faith when I struggled with fear and doubt. As I penned this book, I sought their advice. I've been honoured to share their stories and their wisdom in these pages.

Two are better than one, because they have a good return for their labor: if either of them falls down, one can help the other up. But pity anyone who falls and has no one to help them up.
- Ecclesiastes 4:9-10

These women have come into my life over the past few years and filled my heart with so much love, while people that I thought would be celebrating my success with me are no longer a part of my life. The reality is that not everyone is meant to be with you on your journey. God will move people in and out of your life according to his plan for you. He sends people to take you to the next level in life or help you understand his purpose for you. We need to do our part by practicing discernment to protect our peace, our heart, and our destinies.

THE WHEAT FROM THE CHAFF

It is not always easy to tell who you should be keeping close to you. Things like love, nostalgia, obligation, and the desire to be accepted can cloud our judgment and make it difficult for us to discern who truly supports us and our purpose and who is not a good fit for us on our journey. There is an excellent sermon by Bishop TD Jakes on the three kinds of friends we may encounter. The first is the 'constituents' – people who are more interested in your achievements and work than they are in you. Their support is dependent on how well you are doing. The second kind is the 'comrades' – friends who only have one thing in common with you: a shared problem, concern, or enemy. They don't love you, they just dislike the same thing you do. The third kind of friend—and the kind we should be looking for—is the 'confidants.' Confidants are the friends who are for you, whether you're doing well or poorly. They will celebrate your success, mourn your losses, and invest in your growth. Like Jonathan and David, your friendship will be built on genuine love.

Here are some things to keep in mind when determining who you allow to hold space in your life.

» **Measure by God's word**

Pastor John Thompson, founder of Family Shepherd Ministries, offered this wise advice on practicing discernment in relationships: "When we are born again by faith in the Lord Jesus Christ, God gave us a jeweler's eye, an insight into Scripture in order to discern truth from error, good from evil, right from wrong, wisdom from folly, clean from unclean, God's ways from the world's ways – by means of testing everything by Scripture." [1]

If we use God's word as our measuring stick for friendship, we can identify who has godly character and pure intentions. We can examine friendships like David and Jonathan [2], Elijah and Elisha[3] , and Ruth and Naomi[4] . Each of these pairs demonstrated the kind of loyalty and support you can expect to find in genuine friendship. There was no jealousy or bitterness, they exchanged wisdom, and stood by each other's sides in joyful moments and difficult ones. This is what our friendships should look like.

» **Assign roles**

Not all friendships are made equal. While I love everyone in my life dearly, there are some people I would share my deepest darkest secrets with, some I turn to for advice or direction, and others

---

1 A Call to Discernment: Relationships God's Way" – Family Shepherd Online
2 1 Samuel 18
3 2 Kings 2
4 Book of Ruth

that I have a more superficial connection with. It's like shelves in a pantry. You place people in different places in your life. For example, if you meet someone new, you might put them on the bottom shelf. As the friendship is tested, you can then determine what role they are best suited to play in your life. Are they a confidant, a mentor, a casual friend? Carefully consider the people around you and how they align with different parts of your life and build your relationships accordingly.

» **Lead by example**

If we want healthy and supportive relationships, we have to practice the behaviours we expect from others. Show your friends support, pray for them, be happy for their successes, and be kind to them as they navigate challenges. As we demonstrate the kind of treatment we like, not only do we welcome it into our lives, but it becomes easier to realize when it isn't being reciprocated.

» **Seek mentors and guides**

Whatever point you are at in your journey, you will always need people who are more mature in their walk. These mentors can share knowledge, help you make wise decisions, and prepare you for challenges they know will come your way. A great biblical example of a woman who found and trusted mentors was Queen Esther [5]. When she was chosen as a candidate to marry King Xerxes, she heeded her uncle Mordecai's advice to keep her nationality a secret. She also trusted the instructions of Hegai, the king's eunuch, on what to bring with her when she went before the king. Because she followed the wisdom of older and wiser people in her life, Xerxes favoured her, and she became Queen. Like Esther, make sure you are building relationships with people who not only support you but give you good advice.

---

5 Esther 2

» **Align with like minds**

It's important that at least some of the people in your life reflect your ambition and vision. If you are purpose-driven, it makes sense that you would surround yourself with people who are of similar mindsets. My friend Stephanie shared with me that she frequently assesses the people in her life in light of her goals and aspirations to see who she can rely on to help push her forward in her purpose. I think it's a great idea. Proverbs 13:20 says, "Walk with the wise and become wise, for a companion of fools suffers harm." While not all of our relationships will serve this purpose, we should make sure that we align with people who are walking in the same direction we are and can help us on our path.

» **Watch for God's moves**

This is perhaps the most important method of discernment. God is going to place people in your life. Sometimes you will not understand why, but if the Spirit moves you toward someone, trust that there is a reason. I remember when I first met Angella in a Facebook group. We had not had any significant exchanges, and I had no real reason to reach out to her, but I felt the Holy Spirit tell me to ask for an Angella. The urge was so strong, I posted in the group asking if there was a woman with that name. It took her a long time to respond, and she was reluctant at first, but I felt compelled to keep reaching out to her. The very first time we spoke, she prayed and prophesied over me. She has been an incredible confidant and sister to me ever since. Always keep your eyes and heart open for the people God will bring into your life, and when He pushes you toward someone, follow His direction without hesitation.

Once we know how to identify healthy and supportive relationships, what can we do when we realize someone in our life doesn't fit the bill?

LET GO AND LET GOD

There have been a number of relationships in my life that became toxic and drained my spirit. Sometimes, those terrible relationships were with the people I loved the most. I have shared with you the tumultuous experience I had with my mother. Though I loved her with all my heart and wanted nothing more than to be accepted by her, she rejected and belittled me. The older I grew, and the more God led me to my destiny, the more hateful she became. It took me some time to realize it, but her anger towards me came from her frustration with herself. When she came to Canada as a young woman, she did not make wise use of her time and did not take the opportunity to make something of herself. I realized she envied me for going to school, chasing my career goals, starting a family, purchasing a home, and living a fulfilled life. Her jealousy made her so angry towards me that she even threatened to kill me.

For a very long time, I still felt obligated to try to have a close relationship with my mother despite the way she treated me. I didn't feel it was right for me to walk away from our relationship. I was very distressed by the whole situation and many nights I would wake up in tears. I finally realized that if I wanted to be a good mother to my children, I would need to love my mother from a distance. I made the decision to let my mother out of my life with grace. I do not hate her or wish ill on her. In fact, I love her very much, but I cannot afford to give her my space, energy and time. I am much more at peace now for having made that choice.

If there is someone in your life who you feel obligated to be-cause they are a relative or a long-time friend, but their presence in your life is bad for your spiritual wellbeing and your journey, it is okay to gracefully let go of that relationship. Forgive them, move on, and love them from a distance. I realize making that decision is not easy. That is why I struggled so long to sever the relationship with my mother, but in those difficult moments where I felt lonely and the loss seemed overwhelming, I remembered that I had the ultimate friend in Jesus. As David said in Psalm 27:10, "Though my father and mother forsake me, the Lord will receive me." God does not ever abandon us, and for all the toxic relationships He removes from our lives, we can be confident that He will replace them with people who truly love and care for us.

When all else fails, know that God is the ultimate friend. Every challenge you've overcome and every great thing you have ever achieved has been through His love for you. In your loneliest moments, He was there. In your dark hours, He gave you light. When the road seemed too long, and you felt too tired, He carried you. It is through His grace that you have reached as far as you have, and it will be through His loving support that you will continue to walk in the purpose and destiny that He chose for you.

REFLECTION MOMENT

Complete these exercises

1. Are the relationships in your life serving you? If any are not, examine why you are afraid to let them go.

____

____

____

____

____

____

____

____

____

____

____

2. At this stage of your life, what kind of support do you need? Are your current relationships fulfilling those needs? If not, where can you seek those kinds of relationships?

____

____

____

____

____

____

____

____

____

____

____

3. If you are struggling with gracefully letting go of a toxic relationship, meditate on this scripture:

"All my enemies whisper together against me; they imagine the worst for me, saying, 'A vile disease has afflicted him' he will never get up from the place where he lies.' Even my close friend, someone I trusted, one who shared my bread, has turned against me. But may you have mercy on me, Lord; raise me up, that I may repay them. I know that you are pleased with me, for my enemy does not triumph over me. Because of my integrity, you uphold me and set me in your presence forever."

Psalm 41:7-12

www.ingramcontent.com/pod-product-compliance
Lightning Source LLC
Chambersburg PA
CBHW060946050726
47592CB00003B/1129